Machine
EMBROIDERY
Makes the Quilt

• 6 Creative Projects • CD with 26 Designs
• Unleash Your Embroidery Machine's Potential

PATTY ALBIN

C&T PUBLISHING

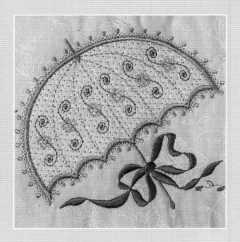

Text © 2004 Patty Albin

Artwork © 2004 C&T Publishing, Inc.

Publisher: Amy Marson

Editorial Director: Gailen Runge

Acquisitions Editor: Jan Grigsby

Editor: Lynn Koolish

Technical Editors: Sara Kate MacFarland, Elizabeth Tisinger

Copyeditor/Proofreader: Wordfirm Inc.

Cover Designer: Kristen Yenche

Design Director/Book Designer: Rose Sheifer

Illustrator: Timothy Manibusan

Production Assistant: Matt Allen

Photography: Luke Mulks and Kirstie McCormick, except as noted

Published by C&T Publishing, Inc., P.O. Box 1456, Lafayette, California 94549

Front cover: Double Wedding Ring by Patty Albin

Back cover: Posy of Pansies by Patty Albin, Holly and Roses Table Runner by Marcia Pollard, and Baltimore Album by Betty Barns

Library of Congress Cataloging-in-Publication Data

Albin, Patty.
  Machine embroidery makes the quilt : 6 creative projects : CD with 26 designs : unleash your embroidery machine's potential / Patty Albin.
    p. cm.
  Includes bibliographical references and index.
  ISBN 1-57120-266-8 (paper trade)
  1. Embroidery, Machine—Patterns. 2. Quilting—Patterns. I. Title.

TT772.A43 2004
746.44'028—dc22

2004007539

Printed in China
10 9 8 7 6 5 4 3 2 1

Table of Contents

Dedication

This book is lovingly dedicated to the two shining lights in my life, my husband Chuck and my daughter Lindsey. With your love and support all things are possible.

Acknowledgments

You wouldn't be reading this book without the support of many people.

Chuck and Lindsey, you inspire me to reach for the stars.

My friend Faun Lee: You proofread the text and patterns, offered me tips and suggestions, talked about the book during our exercise sessions, and never once complained—thank you. This now calls for tiaras, martinis, shopping, and a road trip, although not necessarily in that order.

Terry Smith: You saw and believed in my talent when others, including me, didn't. Thank you for your constant encouragement.

Viking Distributing Company, Inc.; Sylvia Design sewing furniture and Laurastar ironing systems; Sue Hausmann for all her help and support along the way; The Erlanger Group for all their wonderful fabrics; VSM Inc.; Betty Barnes and Wallace Sewing Chalet in Boulder, Colorado, for getting me hooked on all of this to begin with; Debbie Barnisin for her editing of my preliminary writing; Karen Hinrichs for her truly amazing designs; Gwen Woodard, Cindy Swainson, and Trinity Boss for helping to prepare quilts and samples, pattern check numbers, and provide technical information and creative inspiration; The Martha Pullen Company for the embroidery disks; Scrigby's Embroidery Designs for the beeauuutiful doily created for the book; Rhonda Anderson and Tomorrow's Heirlooms in Westminster, Colorado, for their enthusiasm; Sulky of America for the cotton thread; AAA Creative Sewing Center; The Presser Foot in Longmont, Colorado; and the digitizer of my designs —thank you, thank you, thank you.

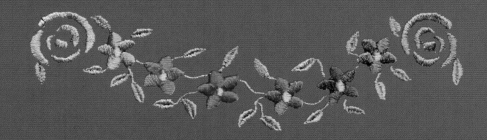

GETTING STARTED

Did you buy an embroidery machine because you thought it would be fun, only to become a little overwhelmed by all those wonderful designs? Maybe you've been using embroideries but have never considered using them in your quilts. Perhaps you are already using machine embroidery in your quilts, but now you'd like a little inspiration and some ideas to use it more creatively.

Then this is the book for you. It's designed to inspire you to use your embroidery machine in ways you've never thought possible. It shows you how to make quilts like those gorgeous ones your friends have made or those quilts you've seen in photos. If you're ready to try something new but don't know where to begin—don't worry. It's easy once you know how.

In addition to ideas and inspiration, this book includes projects you can make by following the instructions and using the included preprogrammed embroideries. Simply transfer the designs from the enclosed CD to a card, disk, or other format that your embroidery machine can read.

The projects range from placing embroideries in traditional quilt blocks to creating the quilt block design entirely with embroidery. You can even create an entire quilt just using machine embroidery.

You do need to know how to use your embroidery machine, including transferring designs, positioning the hoop, knowing what to do if your thread breaks, and so on. If you're not comfortable using your machine yet, you can acquaint yourself with these functions by consulting your manual and taking classes. This book will help you with everything else.

So, if you're ready to start but you'd like a little hand-holding along the way, this book is what you need. You'll find a wealth of creative inspiration to kick-start your imagination. You'll also find a different way to think, new ways to look at your machine and the embroideries you have available to you, and creative ways to use those embroideries in your quilts.

Start now and set off on your own creative journey!

Sources of Inspiration

A good way to start thinking about more ways to use embroidery is to look around for sources of inspiration. Books, magazines, and quilt shows are excellent places to start. As you look at quilts, think about how you might be able to use embroideries in them. Could you add embroideries as accents or embellishments? What embroidery designs would complement a specific type of quilt? Look carefully to see how different quiltmakers use appliqué, silk ribbon embroidery, hand embroidery, or even miniature quilt blocks, then ask yourself if that technique could be translated into machine embroidery.

USING EMBROIDERY IN QUILTS

Combining Quilting and Embroidery

There are so many ways to use embroidery in quilts! Look at the photographs in this section and read the descriptions of how each quiltmaker decided to use the designs she chose for her quilt. Each of these quilts is a unique creation, presented so you can begin to understand the process and formulate ideas of how you can use embroidery in your quilts. Like all the sources of inspiration available to you, these quilts are presented for ideas and are not to be copied or reproduced.

ACCENTS

As you look at quilts and patterns for inspiration, you might see that the creator of a quilt or writer of a pattern has suggested some sort of accent in the quilt. Think "machine embroidery."

The original pattern for *Baby Roses* came from the book *P.S. I Love You* by Nancy Smith and Lynda Milligan of Possibilities. This quilt, originally designed as a wall quilt (called *Baby Tears* in the book), instructed the quiltmaker to tack a ribbon rose embellishment onto the alternating plain block. Instead, Jill dressed it up by using a small rose embroidery. Jill made this quilt for a baby to use, and by stitching the roses into the quilt, she ensured that a child would not be able to pull off the embellishment.

BABY ROSES, 27" x 39", made by Jill Reed, embroidery design by Husqvarna Viking.

Photo by Sharon Risedorph

MATTIE'S QUILT, 46½" x 53½", made by Kathy Emmel, embroidery designs by Kathy Emmel using her Husqvarna Viking software.

In *Mattie's Quilt*, Kathy Emmel used embroideries to personalize the quilt and make it special. She used her embroidery software to create monograms, embroidered names, places, and dates that are meaningful to her and Mattie's family. The combination of machine embroidery and traditional quilt patterns makes this quilt truly one of a kind.

To further personalize the quilt, Kathy incorporated photo transfer images of family members. Kathy took a style of quilt that has been around since the nineteenth century and brought it into the twenty-first century with grace and beauty.

MEADOW BUTTERFLIES, 27" x 27", pieced and quilted by Lynne Dykema, embellished by Gwen Woodard, embroidery designs by Cactus Punch.

EMBELLISHMENTS

Embroideries don't always have to be stitched directly onto the quilt fabric; they can be stitched onto a background fabric and cut out to be used as embellishments. These freestanding embroideries add dimension to any quilt. You can try this technique yourself using the Posy of Pansies *project on page 58.*

This quilt uses a traditional Snowball block with a focus fabric of butterflies. What makes this quilt different from other Snowball quilts are the machine embroideries used as freestanding designs. These were added as embellishments after the quilt was completely constructed. You have to look closely to see which butterflies are embroideries and which are printed on the fabric—the size and coloring of the embroideries are very similar to those on the fabric. Gwen used her embroidery software to manipulate these designs to replicate the patterns in the fabric. Notice how the freestanding embroidered butterflies mingle with the fabric butterflies and fly off into the borders. Partially removing the water-soluble stabilizer left the embroidery somewhat stiff, so Gwen was able to shape the wings of each butterfly before attaching it to the quilt.

A lovely silk print of an old sewing machine (purchased at a quilt show) provided the starting point for this small quilt. After I finished the quilt, I felt it still needed something. Pansies, like the ones in *Posy of Pansies* (see project on page 58), provided just the right touch. Instead of stitching them directly onto the quilt, I used the pansies as freestanding embellishments. I resized the original pansy design several times, stitched it out in several sizes, and placed them around the sewing machine giving the quilt dimension and a unique touch.

After finishing *The Sewing Room*, I had to laugh, because I've never seen a sewing room like that! So, I took a photo of my sewing machine, in my sewing room, printed it out on fabric, and made another quilt. I found embroidery designs that included buttons, scissors, a measuring tape, and spools of thread. The embroideries were stitched, cut out, and attached in the same manner as the pansies. Now that's a real sewing room!

THE SEWING ROOM, 14½" x 11½", made by Patty Albin, embroidery designs from *Machine Embroidery Makes the Quilt* CD.

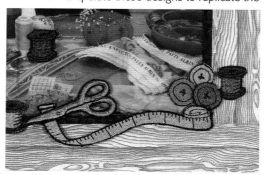

SEWING ROOM REALITY, 14½" x 11½", made by Patty Albin, embroidery designs by Husqvarna Viking, transfer fabric by Color Textiles.

REPLACING APPLIQUÉ

Embroidery is perfect for use in a quilt instead of appliqué. So many quilt designs either incorporate appliqué or have open or alternate blocks that are ideal for embroidery. You can use an embroidery that is very similar to the original appliqué or one that provides a completely different look. The choice is yours. Try this technique yourself with the Irish Chain *project on page 50.*

Beary Good Friends is based on the quilt pattern *Nana's Garden* from *Quilt in a Day.* The original quilt has large open areas in the centers of the blocks that the book suggests be filled with appliqué. Can you think of a better place to use embroidery?

BEARY GOOD FRIENDS, 46" x 46", made by Patty Albin, embroidery designs by Husqvarna Viking.

The Pennsylvania Quilt was inspired by an 1860s antique quilt I saw at a quilt show. The original quilt had an appliquéd block design that looked just like an embroidery design I already had. Within a day, I had my own embroidered interpretation.

THE PENNSYLVANIA QUILT, 16" x 20", made by Patty Albin, embroidery design by Husqvarna Viking.

LOVE AND A LITTLE LUNACY, 24" x 24", made by Faun Lee.

In *Love and a Little Lunacy*, by Around the Block Designs, the quilt is patterned with appliqués, stars, moons, and hearts that all appear in the 4" finished blocks of the quilt. A 4" finished block is the perfect size for many embroideries. In a second version of this quilt, Patrick Lose's embroidery designs are used *instead of* the appliqués. What could be easier?

LOVE AND A LITTLE LUNACY: PATRICK LOSE STYLE, 24" x 24", made by Patty Albin, embroidery designs by Husqvarna Viking.

BALTIMORE ALBUM, 26" x 26", made by Betty Barnes, embroidery designs by Husqvarna Viking.

Before she knew it, Betty had more than enough designs to make a 25-block Baltimore Album quilt with a traditional floral swag border. She drew her inspiration from the photos in the book, used other books as references, and made her own Baltimore Album quilt using the machine embroideries as quilt blocks. You can make your own Baltimore Album-style quilt by using the project instructions starting on page 73.

Electric Baltimore is based on a quilt in the book *Baltimore in Bloom* by Pam Bono, which provides instructions for piecing a large Baltimore Album–style quilt. Betty used one of the author's embroidery cards that has embroideries mimicking these quilt blocks in miniature form. Even the flower petals are angular as in the original pieced blocks. The embroideries provide a way to make the same quilt on a smaller scale.

When working in miniature, it's easy to find or customize embroideries that will work instead of appliqué. In *Baltimore Album*, Betty Barnes used embroideries instead of the appliqués that would have been used to make a traditional Baltimore Album quilt. Betty loves Baltimore Album quilts, and while looking through a book about miniature Baltimore Album quilts, she noticed that the blocks were constructed entirely out of silk ribbon. Betty looked at these designs and thought "machine embroidery."

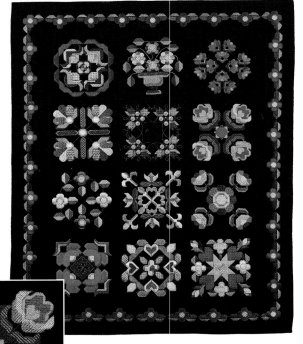

ELECTRIC BALTIMORE, 27" x 32½", made by Betty Barnes, embroidery designs by Pam Bono.

Here are some other quilt block patterns that lend themselves to embroideries instead of traditionally pieced patches.

In some quilt block patterns, you can replace part of the block with an embroidery, but it does take some practice to imagine what a block would look like with some of the elements replaced by embroidery. This technique is what was used in the Redwork *quilt (see project on page 62), in which the inside of the traditional Missouri Puzzle block was replaced with embroidery.*

The inside of a Missouri Puzzle block replaced with embroidery

Hens and Chicks Block

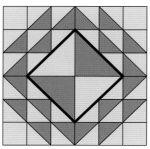

Before

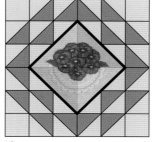

After

Arizona Block

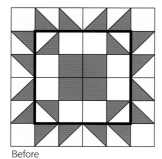

Before

After

Missouri Puzzle Block

Carpenter's Wheel Block

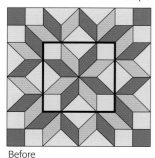

Before

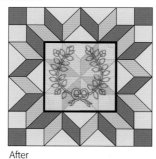

After

Can you see which portion of the Missouri Puzzle block was replaced with an embroidery design?

Old Maid's Puzzle Block

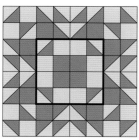

Before

After

REPLACING THE QUILT BLOCK

How about making an entire quilt out of embroideries? There are so many ways to take this approach! Here are just a few ideas.

Using embroidery as the quilt block is a great way to give a traditional quilt a whole new look. *Antique Linens* and *Bows and Lace* use the same basic "grid" and a simple block to create two entirely different, but equally spectacular, quilts.

Bows and Lace caught my eye while Linda was making it, because the embroideries looked *so big*. In reality, each block consists of a number of separate smaller designs that Linda very skillfully combined. Each design could have been stitched out separately, with the fabric precisely re-hooped, but Linda was able to combine designs using her embroidery software. She still had to use a large hoop and hoop multiple times to create such large blocks, but by combining designs, she saved herself some time. Linda also used decorative stitches on her sewing machine to accent the embroidered blocks.

Cindy Losekamp took a similar approach with *Antique Linens*, creating a quilt with a very different look.

BOWS AND LACE, 85" x 85", made by Linda Kopp, embroidery designs by Janny Primrose.

Photo by Sharon Risedorph

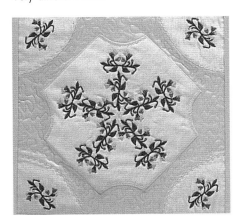

ANTIQUE LINENS, 86" x 86", made by Cindy Losekamp, embroidery designs by Cindy Losekamp.

Photo by Sharon Risedorph

Look at *Garden Party* for yet another approach. The entire quilt is made up of embroideries. I knew I would never cut and piece all the little sections of a traditional Double Wedding Ring arc, so my thoughts turned to embroidery. I designed the flowers to form each arc section so that the patches could be embroidered rather than pieced. If you look closely, you can see that the flowers in the binding are the same flowers as in the rings, only smaller.

GARDEN PARTY, 28" x 28", made by Patty Albin, embroidery designs by Husqvarna Viking.

Karen Hinrichs took my *Garden Party* quilt and made it even better. She wondered, "What would happen if I make the quilt block square and *curve the embroideries* instead?" No curved piecing, only curved embroideries! She used her embroidery software to create flowers and leaves in a curved pattern that looks like the Double Wedding Ring arcs. After embroidering the blocks, she cut out the blocks and sewed them together. Essentially, Karen took the embroidery one step further to make it even easier. You can make your own Double Wedding Ring quilt using the project instructions on page 66.

DOUBLE WEDDING RING, 28" x 28", made by Patty Albin, embroideries designed by Karen Hinrichs. From the *Machine Embroidery Makes the Quilt* CD.

REPLACING HANDWORK

With an embroidery machine, you can easily imitate the look of many hand-embroidery stitches. Some machine embroidery mimics hand embroidery, but when you look closely, you can see it was done by machine. From a normal viewing distance, however, you get the impression *it was* handwork. These designs are not meant to be exact replicas of hand-stitched embroideries; rather they give the illusion they are done by hand. You can make your own hand-stitched creation with the Crazy for You *project (see page 54), which incorporates the features of your twenty-first century embroidery machine and all those beautiful decorative stitches to replicate the look of handwork.*

REDWORK QUILT, 25" x 25", made by Patty Albin, embroidery designs by Patty Albin. From the *Machine Embroidery Makes the Quilt* CD.

Redwork

The popularity of redwork has increased over the past few years. So, it's not surprising to see this enthusiasm carry over to machine embroidery. Look at the examples of stitching done by hand and stitching done by machine. The machine sample was sewn with a 12-weight cotton thread to mimic the hand-sewn one. Can you tell the difference?

Try this technique yourself using the *Redwork, Bluework and Brightwork* Quilt project on page 62. Be sure to use cotton thread to achieve a look similar to hand stitching.

Stitched by hand by Cindy Swainson.　　　Stitched by machine, design by Martha Pullen.

Crochet

I remember my grandmother sitting for hours crocheting lace on the edges of hankies. I loved the look then, and I still do now. With today's time constraints, I turn to my embroidery machine for help. The samples here are from Cindy Losekamp and Scrigby's Designs. Cindy's designs look like the "crocheted lady" pillowcase design of the 1930s.

Look at the crocheted doily by Scrigby's Designs. You have to look *very closely* to see that the work was done by machine. (A few samples of Scrigby's "crocheted" designs were displayed at a trade show. A professional digitizer looked at them closely and deemed them done by hand!) You can make the 6" half-round doily that was designed especially for the *Posy of Pansies* project on page 58.

Machine crochet that looks like hand crochet, by Scrigby's Embroidery Designs

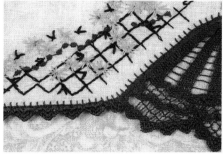

Machine crochet that looks like hand crochet, by Cindy Losekamp

CROCHETED LADY, 14½" x 9", made by Patty Albin, embroidery designs by Cindy Losekamp.

Cross-Stitch and Petit Point

Even cross-stitch and petit point can be done on the machine. You can purchase ready-made designs, plot your own designs, or scan a photo and have software make the design for you.

With cross-stitch software, it's very hard to tell that the work was done on a sewing machine! If you stitch on Aida cloth and get the stitches close to the holes in which a hand cross-stitcher would stitch, most people won't be able to tell the difference.

Machine cross-stitch, with proper hooping and sizing of each 'x,' see how the stitches fall exactly in the holes of the Aida cloth.

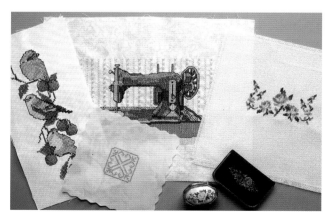

Machine cross-stitch

Bullion Roses

Martha Pullen's embroidery card *Bullion Roses* has embroideries that are digitized to have the appearance of hand-embroidered designs. And from a normal viewing distance, they do!

The photos show a comparison of these machine-stitched roses and hand-stitched roses. My friend Cindy Swainson, an expert hand-embroiderer, embroidered the hand-stitched roses.

Detail of machine-stitched bullion rose

Stitched by hand   Stitched by machine

The machine embroidery isn't supposed to look stitch-for-stitch like the hand stitching. Instead, it should give the appearance and the feel that it might have been done by hand.

Betty Barnes used Jeannie Harrison's *Victorian Dreams* embroidery disk to piece the Crazy Quilt blocks as well as embroider the designs. Martha Pullen's *Bullion Roses* card was also used to embellish Crazy Quilt blocks for Betty's *Crazy Quilt Jacket*. The blocks are embellished with machine embroidery designs, all of which imitate the hand stitching seen in traditional crazy quilting.

In *Baltimore Album*, part of the block was machine embroidered and part of it was embroidered by hand with silk ribbon. How creative!

BALTIMORE ALBUM (detail)
See page 11 for quilt.

CRAZY QUILT JACKET, made by Betty Barnes, embroidery designs by Jeanne Harrison, Bullion Roses by Martha Pullen.

Silk Ribbon

Do you love the look of silk ribbon embroidery but don't like the handwork? Why not combine both kinds of embroideries—silk ribbon and machine? Marcia Pollard has done just that with her own designs that she digitized herself. The *Holly and Roses* designs combine wire ribbon with preprogrammed machine embroideries.

HOLLY AND ROSES TABLE RUNNER,
45" x 18", made by Marcia Pollard,
embroidery designs by Marcia Pollard.

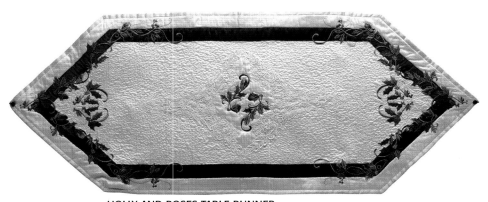

NON-TRADITIONAL QUILTS

Most of what you've seen so far in this chapter has been traditional or traditional-looking quilts in which embroidery was used as an accent, as an embellishment, or as part or all of a quilt block. As you can see, there's no need to limit your imagination.

Gwen Woodard created this quilt using a paper-pieced eagle as the focal interest. What you don't see right away is that this majestic bird is flying over the snow-covered pine trees of Gwen's home in Kenai, Alaska. She embroidered the pine boughs in white and pearlescent white thread. Look closely. Do you see the pinecones hidden among the pine needles?

For this technique, Gwen stitched the pinecones onto nylon organdy. She then cut out the pinecones and appliquéd them onto the background of the quilt. By using machine embroidery and a subtle use of color, Gwen used the raw-edge appliqué technique to give dimension, as well as texture, to the trees. The eagle is free to soar majestically through it all.

QUIET FLIGHT, 52" x 56", made by Gwen Woodard, embroidery designs by Husqvarna Viking, eagle pattern by Brenda Groelz.

SECLUDED SERENITY, 46½" x 36½", made by Cindy Losekamp, embroidery designs by Cindy Losekamp.

COMBINING EMBROIDERY WITH BUILT-IN STITCHES

The artistic combination of photo transfers, appliqués, machine embroidery, and decorative stitches makes this quilt extraordinary. Cindy uses many different techniques to create exactly what she envisions and uses her machine to its utmost potential.

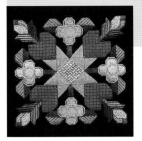

EMBROIDERY DESIGNS

All the embroidery designs you need for the projects in this book are on the included CD. As you expand your collection of embroidery designs, however, you should know what differentiates a good design from a not-so-good design.

What to Look for in Embroidery Designs

High-quality designs are essential for successful embroidery. You can't necessarily tell the quality of an embroidery design by looking at a photograph of the design or even by looking at a computerized image of it. Keep in mind that even a good-quality design can look bad if the fabric isn't stabilized properly or if poor-quality thread is used. That's why it's important to understand what makes a good embroidery design good.

Embroidery designs are created through a process called *digitizing*. A computer is used to indicate the exact position of each stitch in the design, colors are assigned to groups of stitches, and the order in which the design will be stitched is detailed. All of this information is stored in a computerized format for your embroidery machine.

Usually, when designs are digitized for sale to the public, the digitizers have no control over the materials the end user will select. The digitizers have to take into account that the design may be stitched on any type of fabric using whatever type of thread and stabilizer the user chooses.

Here's a guide of what to look for to make sure you are buying high-quality designs.

REGISTRATION

Registration refers to how the colors fit in a design. In embroidery, each color is stitched separately. In a well-digitized design, the colors fit together like a puzzle, are layered one upon the other, or have an outline to separate them. A poorly digitized design can have such inconsistencies as outlines that are off from the body of color or designs that show gaps in the color areas.

JUMP STITCHES

A jump stitch is that long stitch created when the machine moves from one area of the design to another. A good digitizer will consider how to digitize designs so there are few jump stitches to trim and the needed jump stitches are easy to clean up.

Jump stitches are minimized using running stitches.

With good registration, colors fit closely together and outline stitches are exact.

UNDERLAY STITCHING

Good underlay stitching supports the design.

Underlay stitching provides padding and stabilization for an embroidery design and is stitched as the first part of the design. Properly digitized designs have the appropriate kind and amount of underlay stitches to support the design. A design without a good underlay can look puckered, flat, or just not right.

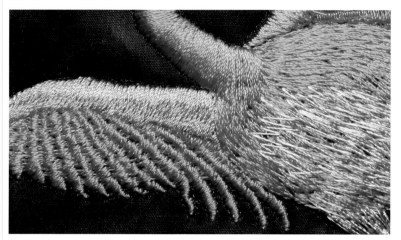

Notice the detail of the feathers in the wings and on the breast. Stitches provide dimension as well as interest.

PINK FLAMINGO, 9 ½" x 11 ¼", made by Patty Albin, embroidery design by Karen Hinrichs.

TEXTURAL INTEREST

Textural interest is provided when different lengths and groups of stitches are used to create different textures within a design. Textural interest may give a sense of shadow or shading, or it may make one area look lighter than another. Different stitch patterns, called fill stitches, also help define different areas of a design.

ELECTRIC BALTIMORE (detail). Look at all the different textures. A variety of fill stitches makes these quilt blocks more interesting. See page 11 for quilt.

Purchasing Designs

It's best to buy your designs from a reputable source. It may help to actually visit a store that sells embroidery designs so you can see stitched-out samples of the different companies' designs. Get recommendations from friends who own embroidery designs. Usually a company's or individual's design quality is consistent. Many embroidery designs are also offered for sale over the Internet, allowing you to immediately download (and use) the designs. Contact information for many sources of designs is listed in Resources (see page 78).

SEWING MACHINE COMPANY DESIGNS

Sewing machine companies that sell embroidery machines also sell embroidery designs. The designs are usually high quality, and if you have any questions, you can talk to the dealer. These companies often license artists to draw the designs for the companies to digitize. This allows names that you know, like Mary Engelbreit, Patrick Lose, or Walt Disney, to provide designs that you can stitch. Due to licensing fees paid to artists, these designs may be more expensive than other designs, but you are assured of high quality.

INDEPENDENT COMPANY DESIGNS

Many companies specialize in creating embroidery designs. Some of the larger companies are Cactus Punch, Dakota Collectibles, Amazing Designs, Oklahoma Embroidery Supply & Design, and EZ Sew Designs—they all produce high-quality designs. These companies offer a variety of design collections. Wanna be a cowgirl? Choose a collection of Western designs. Making kids' quilts? Try juvenile collections. Some of these companies also allow you to purchase one design at a time from their website, so you can buy exactly what you need rather than a packet of designs you don't want.

Some embroidery companies prefer to specialize. For example, some companies sell only monograms and alphabets; others specialize in designs that look like hand-crocheted lace.

Alphabet embroidery cards

INDIVIDUAL DESIGNERS

Buying designs from independent embroidery designers or digitizers can be hit or miss. Many digitizers who want to get their names and designs out for the sewing and embroidery world to buy, sell their designs primarily through the Internet. Some designs are high quality, and some, regrettably, are not. If you or your friends have dealt with a website, and you are familiar with the quality of designs offered there, then by all means use them. Just remember, you often get what you pay for.

Packaged embroidery designs

Copying Designs

When it comes to copyright, there is only one thing you need to know:

When you buy designs (or a book that includes designs), you have purchased the license to use those designs. They are for your use only.

- You cannot copy the designs and give them to your friends.

- You cannot use designs that a friend copied and gave to you.

- You cannot borrow and use designs purchased by someone else, even if you are using the original card or CD.

- You cannot sell items using the purchased designs, unless the packaging specifically states that you may do so.

Copyright violation is a serious matter, and you could be responsible for court costs to defend yourself and pay significant fines. I say the money's better spent on fabrics or chocolate!

EMBROIDERY SOFTWARE

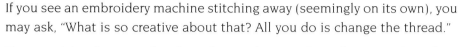

You don't need to own computer software to be creative with your embroidery machine. There are many ways to use the embroidery designs just as they appear on cards or CDs. If you want to take your creativity another step, embroidery software opens the door to limitless possibilities.

If you see an embroidery machine stitching away (seemingly on its own), you may ask, "What is so creative about that? All you do is change the thread."

The creativity doesn't take place during the actual stitching; it takes place *before* or *after* the design has been stitched. Just like selecting your own fabric for a quilt or changing a quilt block pattern, you can change and customize embroidery designs. And, of course, you can always use thread colors different from those specified in the designs.

Notice the difference among the designs. The top is the original design, and the bottom two are the same design modified with embroidery software.

Computers

Whether you already have a computer or are looking to buy one, you should be aware of the following basic hardware and software issues:

- Current embroidery software is Windows-based—it will only work on a computer that uses a Microsoft operating system, such as Windows 98, Windows 2000, Windows XP, and so forth. It won't work on an Apple or Macintosh. If you own an Apple or Mac, read the software packaging carefully.

All software has specific requirements, such as processor speed, memory, and ports, so make sure that the software you want to use will run on the computer you will be using. To make buying software easier, write down a list of the previously mentioned specifics about your computer and keep the list with you so you can refer to it while shopping.

If you are shopping for a computer, purchase the fastest processor and the most memory you can afford. With more memory, your programs will run faster, and you're less likely to run into memory-related problems. You will need a CD-ROM drive, because many companies offer their designs only on CDs. If possible, buy a drive that also writes (or burns) CDs, so you can store your design files on CDs and free up space on your computer.

The 3½" diskette drive is still a necessity, for now. Some embroidery machines still use this format, and designs are often purchased on, or transferred to, diskettes. If your computer doesn't have a built-in diskette drive, external drives are available.

Some of the newer embroidery software requires a USB *port* for a *dongle*. A USB *port* is an "outlet" on the back of the computer where you plug in such devices as a mouse or an external diskette drive. A *dongle* is a device, much like a key, that plugs into a USB port. Some software manufacturers include *dongles* with their software to ensure that the software is being used on only one computer and is not being copied and shared. With this type of software, the *dongle* must be plugged into the computer for the software to be used. If you have several devices that need to be plugged into a USB port, you may need a USB *hub* that lets you plug a number of devices into the same port.

There are many different brands of embroidery software currently on the market. This chapter's goal is to give you information about what types of embroidery software are available so you can learn how much you can do with it. For specific information on using *your* software, consult your manual or ask about training classes at the store where you bought the software.

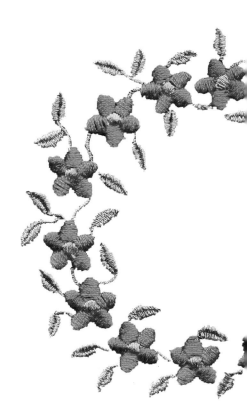

Software

Embroidery software gives you endless possibilities to make or alter your embroidery designs to look exactly the way you want. You should know about the following six types of embroidery software (also called components):

Digitizing and automatic digitizing (auto-digitizing) software—For creating embroidery designs

Customizing and editing software—For combining designs or words or removing elements within the design

Resizing software—For making a design larger or smaller while adjusting stitch density

Format-conversion software—For changing the format, or language, of a design to use it on your machine

Cataloging software—For organizing your designs

Cross-stitch software—For making cross-stitch designs

In *Fractured Saturday,* Gwen helps us remember these old cartoons by combining the characters with televisions and filmstrips to evoke warm feelings and a sense of youth.

As licensed characters, these figures may not appear in any form without the studio's permission. Gwen is able to use the embroidery designs in her quilt because she purchased the embroidery card which gives her the license to use the figures. Notice that as required, the copyright notation is visible in the quilt.

Photo by Roy Mullin

FRACTURED SATURDAY, 54" x 63", made by Gwen Woodard, embroidery designs by Husqvarna Viking.

COPYRIGHT

It's very important to understand that although it's okay for you to make changes to designs you've purchased, it's *not* okay for you to share, trade, or give away any of those changed designs. No *matter how much you've changed them*, the designs are still copyrighted by the original designer, and only *you* have the license to use them. Many designers now specify how their designs can be used (either for personal or commercial use) and state those limitations on the package. Often, when you download designs from the Internet, you must agree to the designer's terms and limitations before proceeding with the installation. Read the fine print on your design packs, and take any copyright symbols or statements very seriously. If a design has a trademark or copyright digitized into it, you *must* stitch that out as well. To purposely eliminate that part of the design is copyright infringement.

Just like embroidery designs, the software that you buy to create or manipulate designs is also protected by copyright laws and is intended for installation on a single computer. *You cannot share or lend your embroidery software.*

BUYING SOFTWARE

Embroidery software may be sold separately or in a bundle—a package with more than one component. Software packages are available that contain all, or almost all, of the components listed above. If you are absolutely sure you only want a specific component, you may want to buy it separately, but overall it is usually less expensive to buy bundled embroidery software packages.

Individual software components

Embroidery software package, or bundled software

Some of the different embroidery components do similar things, or one may sound a bit like another. Talk with the salespeople at the store where you plan to buy, or have already purchased, your software to find answers to your specific questions. It's also a good idea to ask for a demonstration before purchasing, so you can see how the software actually works.

When buying software, don't base your decision only on the lowest price. Instead, evaluate which software has the best features, and consider whether training is available. You also need to be sure that the software will run on your computer.

Yes, it's best to take classes to learn to use the software. If none are available, use the instruction manual and work completely through all the chapters. If you have Internet access, most of the software programs now have online support groups that are usually good sources of information and help.

Software components and bundles are available from various companies and sources.

TYPES OF SOFTWARE

Digitizing and Automatic Digitizing Software

Digitizing is an exciting process because it allows you to create your own embroidery designs—the ultimate in creativity. You determine *exactly* how you want the design to look. You control the placement and size of the stitches as well as the textures and patterns the stitches form.

You can control every aspect of the embroidery design, or you can use auto-digitizing software, which does all the work for you. Auto-digitizing still allows you to make changes to the designs. The choice is yours.

Automatic digitizing software

Special embroidery software now allows you to embroider just about anything you want to say.

With auto-digitizing software, you can create lettering using computer fonts. You simply type your words and choose how big you want the letters to be. The software then creates an embroidery design that you can stitch out on your embroidery machine.

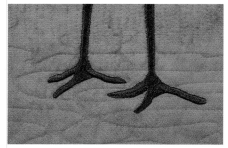

KAREN'S CRANE (details)

Karen's Crane was conceived by Karen Hinrichs and her artistic imagination. She used a photograph of a large crane and digitized it as an extremely large machine embroidery. This quilt *is* the embroidery, which is why it is so extraordinary.

This quilt is a good example of the possibilities available when you digitize your own designs. When Karen agreed to be a parent volunteer for her preschooler's class trip to the zoo, she took her camera with her. She snapped many photos of interesting birds. She later digitized designs based on her photographs.

Look at the details in the feathers and how they appear to flow. The feathers on the breast of the bird are done in two layers. The first layer of feathers prepares the underlay; the second adds the feather texture. Even the feet are detailed to show shape and dimension.

Karen is a very experienced and skilled digitizer. It takes time to learn to create designs with this level of detail. Start simple, and you too can gain experience and learn to create your own spectacular designs.

KAREN'S CRANE, 12" x 21", made by Patty Albin, embroidery design by Karen Hinrichs.

A POND'S LIFE, 123" x 63", made by Kathy Emmel and her students.

A Lesson in Digitizing

To give you an idea of available options when you digitize your own designs, look at *A Pond's Life* by Kathy Emmel. Kathy teaches elementary school and knows that kids learn more by being involved and by doing things they find fun. Every year, Kathy plans a quilt around a lesson she is teaching her fifth-grade students. This particular quilt was based on the life in a pond.

First, Kathy had the students design the quilt as they would like to see it. They had to cooperate and work together, mixing ideas and visions. They also had to draw individual pictures of all the different creatures and plants that lived in and around the pond. Kathy scanned more than 24 sketches that the kids drew for this quilt and then used digitizing software to turn the sketches into embroidery designs.

Original sketch   Digitized embroidery design

For the background, her students painted a big piece of fabric with the pond scene. Then they decided where to place their own designs and took turns at the sewing machine to stitch out the designs.

The software allowed Kathy's class to make this original, educational, and fun quilt. It wouldn't have been nearly as much fun learning about the life in a pond if the kids hadn't been involved in sketching pictures and stitching out designs. Software made it possible.

Stitching out the designs

Patty's Pointers

If you are new to digitizing, auto-digitizing is a good place to start.

To show how easy auto-digitizing is, I took a digital photo of my daughter Lindsey, and saved it in a language my auto-digitizing program understands—in this case, a bitmap. In the software program, I clicked on the button to digitize the picture, and the software created a design that I could then stitch out on my embroidery machine. That's how easy it is.

Auto-digitized design   Original photograph

Customizing and Editing Software

Short of digitizing your own designs, customizing and editing can provide considerable flexibility in working with embroidery designs.

Editing is a form of customizing, and customizing can be a form of editing. These terms can be confusing; make sure the features you want are offered in the program you purchase.

Some examples of customizing are

- Adding words to designs.
- Combining two designs into one design.

Some examples of editing are

- Removing some flowers from a basket.
- Adding or removing color stops or stitches.

In a bundled package, customizing and editing are normally included as part of the package. If you buy the programs separately, check the specifics of each program to make sure you know what is and is not included. Software varies by manufacturer, so before you buy, make sure you understand exactly what you want your software to do. Then find the programs that allow you to do it.

Beary Good Friends (see page 9 for quilt) is a good example of how to use customizing software to make embroidery easier.

This quilt has open areas that are perfect for embellishing with machine embroidery. The blocks are cut on grain (the straight sides of the block follow the straight grain of the fabric) but are set into the quilt on point. Hooping fabric on the bias can be difficult because the fabric tends to stretch and distort along the edges of the hoop. With customizing software, you can hoop the fabric on the straight of the grain and then rotate the

embroidery. For this quilt, each bear was brought up on the computer screen and rotated 45° so it could be stitched out in the proper orientation. Some sewing machines have a built-in rotating option, so you may not even need separate software to rotate designs.

The fabric is hooped on the straight of the grain, and the bear is rotated 45°.

Garden Party (see page 14 for quilt) is another example of using editing and customizing software.

For this quilt, I selected an embroidery design with various flowers. I then used an editing function to isolate individual flowers and place them in the rings.

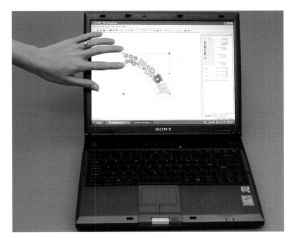

Flowers are placed in an arc on the computer screen with the aid of a curved template that is also used for cutting.

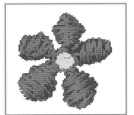  

Individual flowers are selected.

Original designs before editing

I saved each flower and resized it using resizing software (see page 30). I then used the customizing function to place all the individual flowers into an arc.

Each arc section was designed to have a different flower embroidery that would look like fabric. The arc could be stitched out as many times as needed. Using templates, I cut out the embroideries and stitched them together to construct the quilt. The creative portion of this quilt wasn't in the actual stitching out of the embroideries but rather in the process by which the quilt was developed and created within the software.

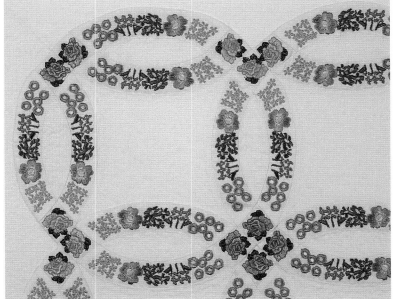

Flowers placed in an arc

When using embroidery software, you will need to know the difference between *rotating* a design and *reversing* a design.

It is possible to rotate or reverse your designs by using computer software or by manipulating the designs directly on your embroidery machine. A rotated design is simply turned in different directions. A reversed design is a mirror image of the original.

ROTATING

Here are four different rotations of the word DIAMONDS. Notice that you can always read the word; it is just in different positions.

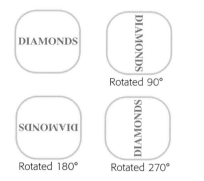

REVERSING

Reversing means to create a mirror image. There are two ways to reverse or mirror a design: side-to-side and top-to-bottom.

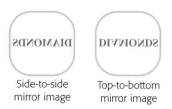

A design that is mirror-imaged may also be rotated. There are several reasons to rotate and reverse designs: Doing so makes a design look completely different, giving you many design looks. It also allows you to fit a design into a specific space in a particular orientation.

Resizing Software

Resizing software allows you to change the size of a design while maintaining the stitch density. If you reduce the size of a design without using this special software, the number of stitches remains the same and the stitched-out design may feel stiff and hard because the stitches are closer together. Conversely, if you make the design larger, the density becomes lower, and you risk having gaps between stitches in the design. Resizing software adjusts the number of stitches to maintain the original stitch density and integrity.

In *Garden Party*, the small flowers on the binding are reduced versions of the flowers in the arcs. I used resizing software so the flowers would be small enough to stitch out on the binding and so the number of stitches would be adjusted to maintain the proper stitch density. The small flowers add a nice complement and a visual edge to the quilt.

The flowers in the binding complement the flowers in the arcs.

Color Sorting Software

Color sorting software is an absolute time-saver. It determines if there are colors in an embroidery design that can be combined to eliminate thread changes. If so, it combines all the colors that are the same and reduces the number of times you have to change the thread. Check the software that you are thinking about purchasing, as this feature may be contained within other components you might already own or are planning to buy.

Format Conversion Software

Format conversion software allows you to convert a design from a format that your machine can't use to one that it can. For example, if you own an embroidery machine by Janome or Brother, you can still use software by another sewing machine company, because the format conversion software lets you save designs (your own or purchased) in the language you need. Some software brands have this component within another program, making this stand-alone component unnecessary. If this feature is something that appeals to you, check the software specifications before you purchase.

The following chart lists design formats and the corresponding sewing machine brands.

EMBROIDERY FORMATS

.ART	Bernina
.CSD	Singer EU
.DST	Tajima
.EXP	DOS Expanded
.HUS	Husqvarna Viking
.JEF	Janome/New Home
.PCS	Pfaff
.PES	Baby Lock, Bernina Deco, Brother
.SEW	Elna, Janome/New Home, Kenmore
.VIP	Husqvarna Viking
.XXX	Singer

Patty's Pointers

For *Garden Party,* I took one arc with fifteen thread-color changes and copied it four times to stitch out in my large hoop. I was able to stitch out four arcs at a time instead of one (that's the advantage of using larger hoops), and I used a thread-color sorting program to reduce the number of thread changes from 60 to15!

This feature saved me time because it eliminated 45 thread changes! It can save you time, too.

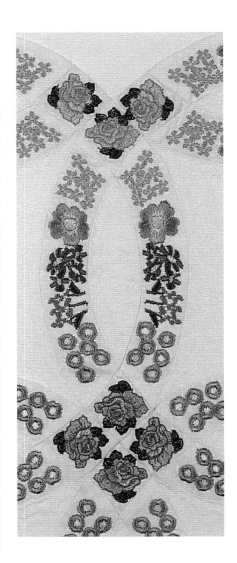

Cataloging Software

Cataloging software helps you organize your designs and even lets you view the designs in folders on your computer. You can view the design image and technical information on your screen, or you can print it out. Cataloging keeps you organized—the more embroidery designs you collect, the more you'll appreciate this type of software.

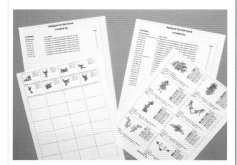

Printouts of your design catalog

Cross-Stitch Software

Cross-stitch software allows you to do two things: You can scan a photo and let the software create a cross-stitch embroidery design, or you can plot your own design (or a design from a purchased cross-stitch pattern).

So get out all those cross-stitch patterns you own, because now you can plot those patterns on your computer and stitch them out on your sewing machine!

FAT QUARTER FRENCH QUARTER (detail), 20" x 20", made by Betty Barnes, cross-stitch design by Rose Mary Le Blanc Barton.

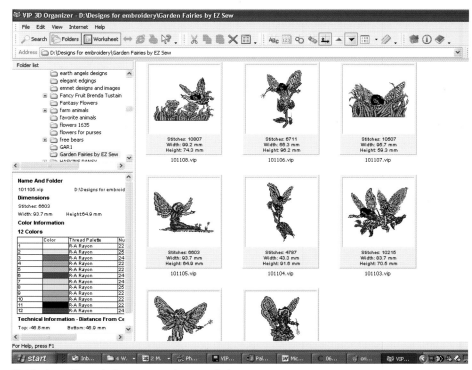

Cataloging software helps you organize your designs.

Photos turned into cross-stitch designs, made by Ericka D. Suhrbier

Cross-stitch embroidery designs

Putting Software to Good Use

Here's an example of how to use the different software components. Look at *Baltimore Album* (see page 11), made by Betty Barnes.

Baltimore Album quilts traditionally have a variety of blocks that represent different aspects of the quilter's, or the recipient's, life. Some blocks are designed specifically for this type of quilt; others, such as the Crossed Laurel Leaves, Basket of Flowers, or Floral Wreaths, are very traditional and appear in many album quilts.

Betty wanted to make a special quilt that meant something to her, so she studied antique Baltimore Albums to get a feel for the blocks. To make this special quilt, Betty knew she would be customizing designs, which is where embroidery software came into play.

Original design

If you look closely, you will notice that the leaf is actually a maple leaf, not a grape leaf.

Swirling Grape Leaves block

Single leaf copied eight times to form a circle

The Swirling Grape Leaves block is a Baltimore Album classic, but Betty couldn't find an existing design she liked. She studied the two design elements that made up the block—the grapes and the leaves—and then started looking at embroidery designs she could combine. She found what she was looking for in the Husqvarna Viking embroidery library.

Betty needed the grapes. Although she found many grapes in all different sizes, shapes, and colors, nothing really worked for her. Instead, Betty found something that *would* work. The design she used is actually a blackberry or raspberry. However, because it is stitched out in the colors of grapes and surrounded by leaves that look like grape leaves, the fruit looks like grapes.

Betty then used resizing software so the design would fit within the swirling circle of leaves. She had her "traditional" Baltimore Album block!

Betty used embroidery software and her imagination to create all the blocks for a Baltimore Album quilt that is truly hers.

Betty brought the leaf into the computer program that allows her to customize designs. Copy and Paste work in customizing software just like they do in a word-processing program. To keep the leaves from being stitched out in a haphazard manner, she copied a leaf and pasted it eight times in a circle in the order she wanted them to be stitched.

EMBROIDERED QUILT LABELS

Even after you have a gorgeous quilt, you're not done. You need a quilt label on the back with all the necessary information, such as your name, where you live, when you made it, what embroidery designs you used, and so on.

Embroidered and Handwritten Labels

Consider using an embroidery design in the label. Do you have a leftover embroidery that you didn't use? Use it on the back for the label. If there isn't room to add embroidered lettering, handwrite the information.

Machine-embroidered and handwritten label

Label from **BEARY GOOD FRIENDS**
See page 9 for quilt.

Embroidered Labels

If your embroidery software includes lettering or if you own a lettering software program, you can use it for all the information you want to stitch out. Choose a font that complements the quilt itself. For a child's quilt, use lettering that looks like child's handwriting. If it's a more elegant quilt, choose something that continues that theme.

Label from **FLOWERS FOR LINDSEY**

Label from **MINIATURE BALTIMORE BEAUTY 4**

Embroidered Photo Transfer Labels

A photo transfer label can speak volumes about the quilt. A photo of your child at the age she made or received the quilt is priceless. How about a photo of a family gathering or of the class that made the quilt? Transfer the image onto fabric, hoop it up, and stitch out an embroidery. It makes the back just as special as the front.

Photo transfer and embroidered label

Patty's Pointers

When making a custom quilt label on your machine, be sure to check for typos before you stitch it out. I was in such a hurry to get *Garden Party* mailed to a show, I never checked the quilt label before it was stitched, and there was a doozy of an error. I believe that labels should have enough information (such as your address and phone number) that if the quilt gets lost, it can be returned. If you don't stitch out the correct phone number, it might be a bit difficult for you to be found!

Garden Party
Patty Albin
5667 W. 109th Circle
Westminster, CO 80020
303-465-9147

June 2003

Check label before stitching and sewing onto quilt!

TOOLS AND SUPPLIES

Having the proper materials, tools, and supplies is critical to achieving beautiful embroidery. After you know what's available and how to use it, you'll be able to focus on all the creative ways to use embroideries in your quilts.

There are many types and brands of stabilizers.

Stabilizer

A stabilizer does what its name implies—it stabilizes the fabric for embroidery. It keeps the fabric smooth and flat and helps prevent puckers from being stitched into your work. There are many stabilizers available—some go underneath the fabric, while others go on top; some spray on, soak in, or iron on.

The type of stabilizer you need depends on the style of embroidery you've chosen and the type of fabric on which you will embroider. Selecting a stabilizer can be a personal preference, so try different types and brands to see what works best for you.

TEAR-AWAY STABILIZER

A tear-away type of stabilizer is the most popular for embroidery. If you want to be able to remove the stabilizer from behind the embroidery by simply tearing it away, use this stabilizer. This inexpensive product is easy and fast to remove and provides good stability for light- to medium-weight cotton (the weight of cotton most quilters use).

Tear-away stabilizer is the perfect choice for this embroidery.

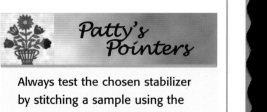

Patty's Pointers

Always test the chosen stabilizer by stitching a sample using the same type of fabric and thread that you will use in the final project. This also gives you the chance to see your thread choices in the finished design. Be sure to test the stabilizer removal method as well to make sure it won't damage the stitches.

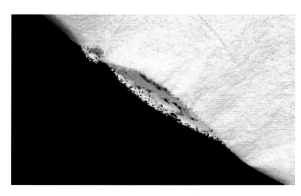

The stabilizer tears away easily without damaging the stitches.

IRON-ON STABILIZER

Iron-on stabilizer usually has a waxlike film on one side that is ironed onto the *wrong* side of the fabric. This is a good choice for lightweight fabrics, which have a tendency to shift or stretch in the hoop. With this stabilizer, the fabric can't shift because the entire piece of fabric is secured onto the stabilizer. After the embroidery is complete, the stabilizer can be peeled or torn away.

WATER-SOLUBLE STABILIZER

Water-soluble stabilizers are a good choice for intricate designs where it may be hard to tear away the stabilizer. Rather than using a stiletto or seam ripper to get into the small spaces to remove bits of stabilizer, all you need to do with a water-soluble stabilizer is cut or tear away excess stabilizer and then dissolve the rest in water.

Water-soluble stabilizers can be used on top of, as well as underneath, fabric. When using water-soluble stabilizer on top of the fabric, it is especially important to do a test sample to make sure all the stabilizer will wash or rinse away. Agitating lightly by hand in warm water sometimes expedites the process. This is the best choice for designs that have large open areas, such as crochet or lace.

Water-soluble stabilizer that disappears completely

STICKY-BACK STABILIZER

Sticky-back stabilizer, which is sticky on one side (covered with a protective sheet), is used with fabrics or quilts that can't be hooped. For example, to embroider the corner of a quilt that doesn't have enough fabric to be held securely in the hoop, first hoop the sticky-back stabilizer. Once hooped, remove the stabilizer's protective sheet, place the fabric or quilt onto it, and you are ready to embroider.

Patty's Pointers

Water-soluble stabilizers must be rinsed *thoroughly* to remove any residue of the product. If not, the embroidery may have a hard or stiff feel to it. Some water-soluble stabilizers contain fibers that remain in the quilt after the stabilizer binder is washed away. These stabilizers must only be used underneath the fabric on which the embroidery is being stitched. Again, test all products before use, and carefully read the manufacturer's label.

Water-soluble stabilizer (used on the back of the fabric) with fibers still in the stitches

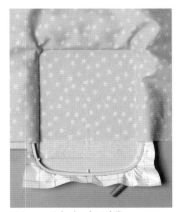

Using a sticky-back stabilizer

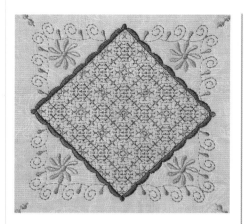

IRON-ON FLEECE

Iron-on fleece is a polyester fleece that you iron onto the back of fabric. This fleece can take the place of batting and should be cut to the same size as the fabric being embroidered. Some quilters and embroiderers use iron-on fleece as a stabilizer because it adds a puffy look to the embroidery (the embroidery is stitched through the fabric and the batting at the same time).

The fleece becomes part of the quilt. When constructing a quilt using iron-on fleece as a stabilizer, you must prepare all the quilt blocks with the iron-on fleece, even if some blocks are not embroidered. You may want to iron the seams open to eliminate bulk. You can also use an additional lightweight batting when layering before quilting.

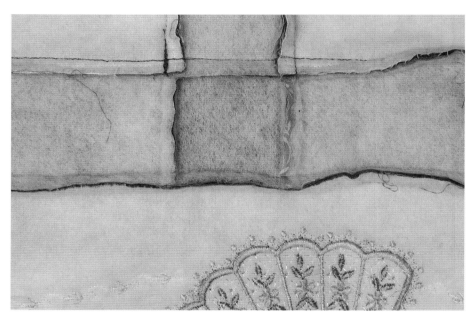

Iron-on fleece used as a stabilizer

HEAT-REMOVABLE STABILIZER

As its name implies, heat-removable stabilizer is removed with the application of heat. Use this type of stabilizer on the back of your embroideries when you prefer not to use a water-soluble or tear-away stabilizer. For example, you may want to use a heat-removable stabilizer for designs with small areas, such as redwork designs. Heat-removable stabilizer is perfect for see-through fabrics that shouldn't get wet or where tear-away stabilizer may remain, causing a shadow within the design. Don't use heat-removable stabilizer on such fabrics as velvet or velveteen, because the heat may melt the fibers or leave permanent marks on the fabric.

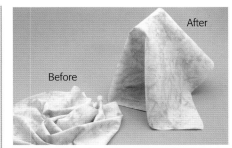

LIQUID STABILIZER

Liquid stabilizer stiffens fabric and may eliminate the need for any other stabilizer. You can also use it in combination with other stabilizers to minimize or eliminate the chance of the hooped fabric shifting or puckering. Saturate the fabric completely with the stabilizer and let it air-dry. Never iron the fabric while it is still wet. You *can* speed the drying process by using a blow-dryer. The liquid stabilizer makes the fabric stiff, so it must be washed out either after the embroidery is finished or after the quilt is assembled. The fabric may appear to have water marks, but they will disappear when you wash the fabric.

Fabric before and after being treated with liquid stabilizer

You can purchase ready-made liquid stabilizer, or you can make your own by dissolving a clear water-soluble stabilizer in a little water. Either way, test to make sure the fabric can be rinsed and the stabilizer removed completely.

Patty's Pointers

I always use liquid stabilizer on my cottons because I want to make sure my fabric is totally stabilized. I prefer to do as much preparation as I can to ensure that there is no shifting during my embroidery. I find liquid stabilizer especially useful when embroidering extremely large designs in a large hoop.

Be sure to test first to make sure there are no surprises when the fabric is rinsed.

With liquid stabilizer, the fabric remains flat.

Without liquid stabilizer, the fabric puckers when stitched.

SPRAY STARCH

Spray starch and spray sizing are fast becoming indispensable for quilting. Many quilters have discovered that when fabric is starched, it's less likely to shift and distort during cutting and sewing. The same is true for embroidery. Although spray starch isn't as stiff as liquid stabilizer, it can help stabilize fabric.

Test any spray adhesive if you are using it with water-soluble stabilizer. A chemical reaction may occur with some stabilizers, making complete removal difficult.

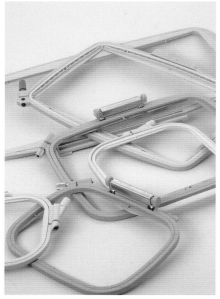

SPRAY ADHESIVE

Although spray adhesive isn't a true stabilizer, it can be used with tear-away stabilizer to create an alternative to sticky-back stabilizer.

Simply spray the adhesive onto a tear-away stabilizer in the hoop or onto the back of the fabric where it will be embroidered. Press the fabric onto the hooped stabilizer. The adhesive will prevent the fabric from shifting on top of the stabilizer. If you are spraying the hooped stabilizer, make a cardboard template to protect the hoop from overspray.

Use spray adhesive to ensure that items you want to incorporate into the embroidery, such as appliqués, ribbons, or other embellishments, stay in place.

Spray adhesives and protective template to protect hoop from overspray

Hoops

Hoops come in many sizes and kinds. All hoops have an inner and an outer piece to hold the fabric and stabilizer (or sometimes just the stabilizer) securely to prevent shifting.

After the fabric and stabilizer are hooped, the hoop is attached to the embroidery arm of the sewing machine. Choose the smallest hoop that accommodates the size of design you have selected. Using a smaller hoop saves on stabilizer and can be easier to use; using a larger hoop allows you to combine designs and saves time by minimizing re-hooping. Most embroidery packaging and machines indicate the size of the embroidery designs, usually in millimeters.

STANDARD HOOP

Most machines come with a hoop that is about 100mm x 100mm (about 4'' x 4''). Many designs can be stitched out in this size hoop.

LARGE OR MEGA HOOP

A larger hoop is needed for large embroidery designs that don't fit in a smaller hoop. You can also combine a number of smaller designs into one big design or make multiple copies of a small embroidery without re-hooping. Combining designs in one hoop means fewer hoopings, which makes it easier for you. Some machines come with a large or mega-size hoop.

Match the size of the design to the size of the hoop.

MINI HOOP

Use a mini hoop for small designs. Mini hoops can be secured tightly and minimize the use of stabilizer. Some manufacturers have a spring-style hoop for this size.

Thread

Many threads are available for you to experiment and be creative. When it comes to thread size (it's actually called *weight*), the *bigger* the number, the *finer* the thread. Pay attention to thread size when selecting thread and needles for different types of embroidery.

There are many types of thread to use for embroidery.

COTTON THREAD

Cotton thread, which is commonly used for piecing and quilting, is available in a wide variety of colors. It is not often the thread of choice for embroidery unless the quilt will be laundered and will experience a lot of use or if a thread with no sheen is desired.

If you want to use cotton thread, try a 60-weight, because this lighter-weight thread doesn't add bulk to the embroideries. If you can't find the color you need in a 60-weight, try a 50-weight instead. Although the 50-weight is a bit heavier, it is worth it for a good color match.

Some designs, such as redwork or crochet, lend themselves to a heavier cotton thread, such as a 25- or 30-weight cotton. This heavier weight gives the illusion that the thread in the embroidery is actually embroidery floss or crochet thread. Be sure to use a larger needle, such as a topstitch needle. (See pages 44–45 for more on needles.)

RAYON THREAD

Rayon is a good choice for embroideries in a wall quilt, art quilt, or any project that *won't* receive a lot of hard wear. Rayon has a very pretty sheen and sews out nicely. Rayon, like cotton, is available in several different weights, including 30- and 40-weight. Most commercially available embroidery designs are designed to be stitched in 40-weight rayon thread.

Rayon is available in a very wide variety of colors and variegations.

IRISH CHAIN (detail), see page 50 for quilt. 50-weight cotton thread used for embroidery

BRIGHTWORK QUILT (detail), see page 65 for quilt. A heavier-weight cotton thread (such as 30-weight) looks more like embroidery floss.

CROCHETED LADY (detail), see page 16 for quilt. 30-weight cotton thread looks like crochet in this design.

A POND'S LIFE (detail), see page 27 for quilt.

BOWS AND LACE (detail), see page 13 for quilt.

POLYESTER THREAD

Polyester thread is strong and is becoming more popular for embroidery. There are many new polyester threads on the market in a widening array of colors and variegations—some have the look and feel of cotton, while others have a feel and sheen similar to rayon.

A 40-weight polyester thread can be used just like a 40-weight rayon thread. The heavier polyesters can really trick the eye when used in an embroidery designed to look like embroidery floss or crochet thread.

When using heavier polyester, make sure you use a size 100 topstitch needle, slow down your machine (many machines have a half- or slow-speed option), and keep the bobbin area free of lint buildup. Otherwise, you might experience thread breakage problems.

METALLIC THREAD

If you have a design that has a fire, flame, halo, or anything that you want to give a bit of a spark, don't forget the metallics! When using these threads, be sure to use a needle made especially for metallic threads. Metallics are decorative and are not recommended for embroideries that will receive hard use.

Embroidery with metallic thread

BOBBIN THREAD

Now that you know what to use on the top of the embroidery, here's what you need to know about the thread used behind the design—the bobbin thread.

To eliminate thread bulk in the embroidery, it is recommended that a thin thread, preferably a 60-weight, be used in the bobbin. Cotton and polyester are very popular choices, and 70-weight lingerie thread is growing in popularity. A finer thread means more thread can be wound on the bobbin, which translates into fewer bobbin changes. Take special note, though, that some of these finer threads may trick the bobbin tension into thinking there is no thread in the tension mechanism. When that happens, the bobbin thread is pulled to the top and is visible within the embroidery—you may need to adjust the tension (either the top or the bobbin). Again, try various weights and fibers to find the ones that work for you.

Needles

To select the correct needle, match the *needle* to the *thread* while keeping in mind your *fabric* choice. Selecting the appropriate needle prevents unnecessary problems. Read on to learn more about the different types of needles. Unlike thread, when it comes to needles, the larger the number, the larger (and stronger) the needle.

NEEDLE SIZES

European	American
60	8
65	9
70	10
75	11
80	12
90	14
100	16
110	18
120	19

EMBROIDERY NEEDLES

Embroidery needles have a special smooth eye that allows smooth thread delivery to the fabric. Embroidery needles are also extremely sharp. These needles split the fabric threads to allow the passage of the needle and thread, which eliminates feathering of the design by preventing the needle from falling on either the right or the left of the fabric thread. Embroidery needles are available in two sizes—75/11 and 90/14. If the smaller size shreds the thread, try the 90/14.

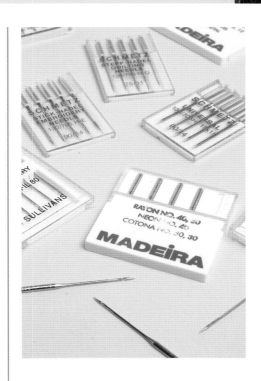

METALLIC NEEDLES

Metallic needles have a larger, heat-tempered eye that allows metallic threads to pass through the eye without heat buildup that may cause shredding and breaking. These needles are sharp like embroidery needles and should always be used with metallic thread. Metallic needles are available in sizes 70/10 through 90/14.

TOPSTITCH NEEDLES

Topstitch needles have large eyes to accommodate heavier threads. The size of the eye and of the shank increases with the size of the needle. Topstitch needles also have a groove in the shank to accommodate heavier threads, such as those used for redwork or machine crochet. Topstitch needles are available in sizes 80/12 through 100/16. If the thread is shredding, try using a larger needle size.

QUILTING NEEDLES

Quilting needles are tapered to penetrate many layers of fabric in a quilt. When quilting, try a needle designed specifically for that purpose. Quilting needles are available in sizes 75/11 and 90/14.

JEANS NEEDLES

Jeans needles are very sharp, have a heavier shank than embroidery needles, and are good for use with heavy woven fabrics. If you are stitching a very dense embroidery, the needle needs to be strong and sharp to penetrate through all the layers of stitches. A jeans needle is a good choice for this type of design if embroidery needles keep breaking. As with the embroidery needle, the jeans needle splits the fabric thread when making the stitch so the stitches appear to have a consistency about them rather than a zigzag. Jeans needles are available in sizes 70/10 through 110/18.

UNIVERSAL NEEDLES

Universal needles can be used on many different types of fabrics because they have a slightly rounded point. Even though they are called "universal," it's best to use a needle designed for the intended use. Universal needles are available in sizes 60/8 through 120/19.

Scissors

You might be surprised at the number and type of specialty scissors available that are perfect for machine embroidery. A good pair of scissors, designed for the task at hand, will save you a great deal of frustration. Whatever type of scissors you prefer, be sure to keep them clean and sharp.

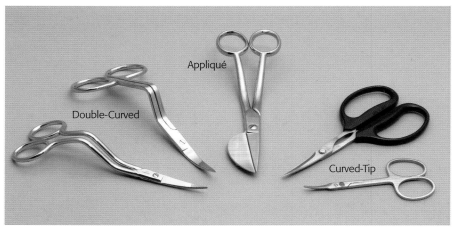

Scissors designed for machine and hand appliqué and embroidery

MACHINE EMBROIDERY SCISSORS

These specialty scissors are available in two styles. Curved-tip scissors have short blades with a slight curve so they fit under the threads for trimming. Double-curved scissors have blades similar to curved-tip, except the handles are curved to fit over the machine embroidery hoop.

APPLIQUÉ SCISSORS

Some embroidery designs require fabric to be cut away once a basting stitch has been used to define an appliqué piece. Appliqué scissors (sometimes called "duck bill" or "pelican bill") make cutting the fabric easier and reduce the risk of cutting into the base fabrics.

Thread Organizer

Several different types of thread organizers are available for holding multiple spools of thread. You may purchase a ready-made organizer, or you can make your own. To make your own, simply pound long nails into a small piece of scrap wood and then number each nail. When you are ready to embroider, place the corresponding spool of thread on each nail. Thread organizers keep your threads ready to stitch in the order they are needed.

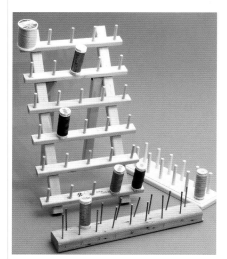

Thread organizers

Projects

Irish Chain

Page 50

Crazy for You

Page 54

Posy of Pansies

Page 58

Redwork, Bluework, and Brightwork Quilt

Page 62

Double Wedding Ring

Page 66

Miniature Baltimore Album

Page 73

Please read these general guidelines and all of the instructions for your selected project before beginning a project.

I prefer to use Perfect Sew liquid stabilizer or spray starch on the fabric I am going to embroider. I believe the added body helps eliminate puckers and shifting while stitching. I suggest you try it to see if it works for you. I also use a stabilizer underneath the fabric, as needed. The specific project instructions indicate the type of stabilizer that is best for each quilt.

Before You Start

All of the designs for the projects are included in the CD at the back of the book. You will need to transfer the designs to a card, disk, or other format that your embroidery machine can read.

BOBBINS

It's a good idea to fill bobbins for your project *before* you start, because it is often time-consuming and inconvenient to stop to fill bobbins during a project. (See Bobbin Thread on page 44 for more information.)

TEST STITCHING

Test stitch all the embroideries for a project *before* you use them in the actual project. This allows you to see how the thread color and weight will work with the fabric and stabilizers you plan to use.

Each embroidery design has a thread color order that is specific to that design. You may choose colors other than those indicated by the embroidery; just make sure the threads are in the proper order so you don't stitch out blue leaves and green flowers (unless, of course, you want to). Test stitching is particularly important in terms of colors, as it gives you a chance to see the order in which the design will be stitched and you can plan your color selections. You can also see if you like the combination of colors you've chosen.

The yardage given at the beginning of each project allows *an extra ½ yard* of embroidery background fabric for you to test the embroideries, stabilizers, and thread colors. This may seem like a lot of extra fabric, but you'll want to stitch out a few embroideries first to make sure the colors you've chosen go well with the quilt fabric and that the stabilizer is providing the needed support. This is also a good opportunity to try out Perfect Sew or spray starch.

HOOPING

When doing multiple embroideries for a quilt, I don't precut my fabric for each embroidery. Instead, I find it easier to hoop a larger piece of fabric, such as a fat quarter. You may find it helpful to mark the centers of the blocks with a small centering "+" using a water-soluble marker before you begin to embroider.

When hooping, be sure to leave enough space between embroideries to center them and cut them out as needed. *Remember that your fabric will draw up during the embroidery process.* Do not cut fabric to the exact measurement you need, because the final dimensions will be smaller or distorted by the embroidery; always cut more than you need. Embroider, press, then trim fabric to size.

POSITIONING POINTS

Marking positioning points on your fabric will help you place the fabric and the embroidery design precisely where you want them. Determine where on the fabric the embroidery should be positioned, then hoop the fabric accordingly.

If you have marked the fabric in any way, you must remove all markings before pressing as the heat will set those positioning marks!

Pressing

When it comes to pressing embroideries, special care should be taken. Pressing down too hard directly on an embroidery makes the threads in the embroidery appear flat and smooth rather than three-dimensional. Press from the *back*, with the embroidery face down on a soft surface, such as a towel, a piece of batting, or a well-padded ironing board cover. This will keep the iron from affecting the embroidery. Always *press gently*, and *never drag* your iron across an embroidery; dragging causes distortion of both the embroidery and the fabric.

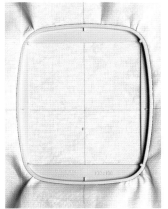

Mark the fabric with positioning lines, note the positioning points on the embroidery hoop, and align the marked fabric with the positioning points on the hoop.

Do not press an embroidered design directly on the right side of the fabric.

Do press the design on the wrong side of the fabric.

If you've stitched puckers into your embroidery, no amount of pressing will iron them out. If you don't preshrink your fabric before embroidering and then you dampen the fabric or embroidery (some quilters use a spray bottle of water while ironing) and press it immediately, you run the risk of shrinking the fabric and causing the embroidery to pucker. Use only a dry iron to press your embroideries.

Finally, always press your embroideries *before* trimming them down to the specified size for your quilt. This ensures that the embroidery and the fabric are nice and flat *and* appropriately sized before and after trimming.

Pressing won't fix the mistake of poor stabilization that results in puckers.

Irish Chain

Made by Patty Albin

Finished quilt size:
26¼" x 26¼"

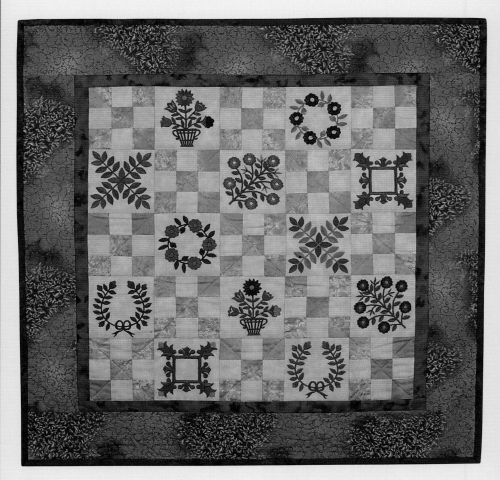

This quilt is fast, easy, and fun. For a consistent look, match the threads in the embroideries to the colors in your border fabric.

Please read the project guidelines on pages 48–49 before beginning the project.

THREAD ORDER

LAUREL LEAVES
82.6mm x 82.2mm • 11,423 stitches

Supplies

See pages 36–46 for a complete description of embroidery supplies.

FABRICS

- ❏ ⅓ yard dark for darker chain squares
- ❏ 1¾ yards light for embroidery backgrounds and light chain squares
- ❏ ¼ yard for inner border
- ❏ ½ yard for outer border
- ❏ 1 yard for backing
- ❏ ⅓ yard for binding
- ❏ 30" x 30" cotton batting

WREATH
83.1mm x 83.1mm • 7,594 stitches

NOTIONS

- ❏ 50-weight cotton thread for quilt construction
- ❏ Embroidery sewing machine needles
- ❏ Tear-away stabilizer to use under the fabric
- ❏ Assorted threads for embroidery (The pictured quilt is embroidered with 60-weight cotton.)
- ❏ Hoop to accommodate a 100mm x 100mm design (If your hoop size is smaller, you will need to make size adjustments to the design.)

BRANCHES
83.6mm x 83.5mm • 6,897 stitches

BASKET
76.6mm x 84.3mm • 8,498 stitches

EMBROIDERY DESIGNS

- ❏ *Laurel Leaves, Wreath, Branches, Basket, Frame, Flowers* embroideries, transferred from the CD to a card or disk for your machine

FRAME
87mm x 86.9mm • 7,737 stitches

FLOWERS
85.4mm x 85.7mm • 12,099 stitches

Cutting

Darker chain square fabric

- Cut 5 strips 1¾" x width of the fabric for the chain squares.

Light background fabric

- Cut 18" x width of the fabric for test stitching the embroideries (see page 48).
- Cut 4 strips 1¾" x width of the fabric for the chain squares.
- The remaining fabric is for the embroideries.

Inner border fabric

- Cut 2 strips 1¼" x 19¼".
- Cut 2 strips 1¼" x 20¾".

Outer border fabric

- Cut 2 strips 3½" x 20¾".
- Cut 2 strips 3½" x 26¾".

Binding fabric

- Cut binding as needed for your preferred binding method.

Assembly

EMBROIDERY

1. Hoop the background fabric with the tear-away stabilizer. Stitch out 12 embroideries on the background fabric, spacing them so each can be cut out in a 4¼" x 4¼" square.

2. When the stitching is complete, remove the stabilizer and press each embroidery before cutting.

3. Cut out each embroidery, centering it in a 4¼" x 4¼" square.

QUILT ASSEMBLY

Use a scant ¼" seam allowance, unless otherwise noted.

1. Sew together lengthwise the 1¾" strips to make 2 strip sets of dark-light-dark and 1 strip set of light-dark-light. Press the seam allowances toward the dark fabric.

Unit A   Unit B

Make strip sets.

2. Cut 26 A units 1¾'' wide from the dark-light-dark strip sets and 13 B units 1¾'' wide from the light-dark-light strip sets. Assemble the Nine-Patch blocks using 2 A units and 1 B unit. Press.

3. Arrange the Nine-Patch blocks and the embroidered squares as shown. Sew the blocks together. Press the seam allowances for the blocks in adjacent rows in opposite directions so they nest when the rows are sewn together.

4. Sew the rows together. Press the seams in one direction.

5. For the inner border, sew the 19¼''-long strips to each side of the quilt top. Press. Sew the 20¾''-long border strips to the top and bottom of the quilt top. Press.

6. For the outer border, sew the 20¾''-long strips to each side of the quilt top. Press. Sew the 26¾''-long strips to the top and bottom of the quilt top. Press.

7. Layer, baste, and quilt. To accent the chain, use diagonal quilting lines through the Nine-Patch squares. Another option is to quilt around the embroideries. For the borders, stitch in-the-ditch along all seamlines.

8. Square up the quilt using a large square ruler and a rotary cutter.

9. Bind the quilt.

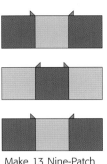

Make 13 Nine-Patch blocks.

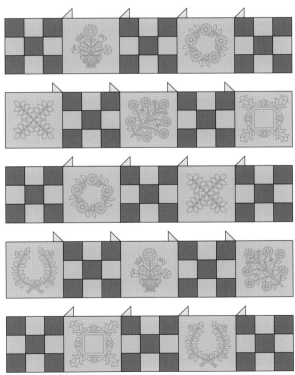

Quilt Assembly Diagram

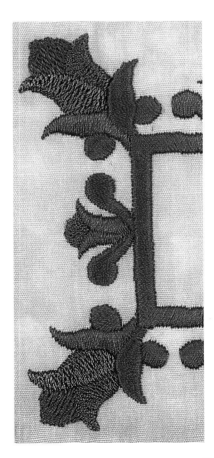

Crazy
for You

Made by Patty Albin

Finished quilt size:
14" x 14"

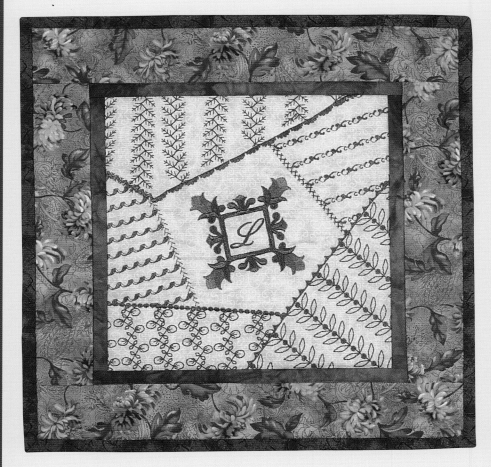

Crazy quilts reached their peak in popularity late in the nineteenth century. To make a Crazy Patch block, quilters pieced different fabrics onto a foundation in a crazy way. Decorative stitches covered the seams of the different fabric patches within the block. Hand-sewn embroideries further embellished the blocks. In the past, decorating these patches and blocks was a time-consuming task, because many of the stitches were elaborate and the embroideries ornate.

Today, you can replicate all of this work with your twenty-first-century sewing machine. You can hoop up the fabric and stitch out the most complicated of embroideries simply by touching a button. Embellish it further using built-in stitches on your machine.

Supplies

See pages 36–46 for a complete description of embroidery supplies.

FABRICS

☐ ½ yard light value tone-on-tone for embroidery background

☐ ¾ yard darker contrast for inner border and binding

☐ ¼ yard complementary floral print for outer border

☐ ⅝ yard for backing

☐ 18" x 18" cotton batting

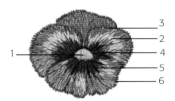

Please read the project guidelines on pages 48–49 before beginning the project.

PANSY
46.0mm x 40.7mm • 4,509 stitches

NOTIONS

❑ *If you are embroidering the doily*: 1 spool (500 yards) white or ecru cotton thread between 50-weight and 30-weight OR

❑ *If you are not embroidering the doily*: One 6''-round Battenberg lace or crocheted doily

❑ 50-weight cotton thread for quilt construction

❑ Seam sealant/fray preventive, such as Fray Check, or wood/stencil burner

❑ Embroidery sewing machine needles

❑ Temporary spray adhesive

❑ Assorted rayon or other decorative threads for embroidery

❑ Monofilament thread (optional)

❑ Water-soluble stabilizer that washes out *completely*

❑ Hoop to accommodate 100mm x 100mm designs or larger (If your hoop size is smaller, you will need to make size adjustments to the design.)

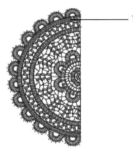

LEAF
17.7mm x 35.1mm • 1,074 stitches

EMBROIDERY DESIGNS

❑ *Pansy*, *Leaf*, and *Doily Half* embroideries (if you have a hoop larger than 100mm x 100mm) or *Doily Quarter* embroidery, transferred from the CD to a card or disk for your machine

DOILY HALF
76.6mm x 149.1mm • 13,580 stitches

Cutting

Corner triangle fabric

▪ Cut 2 squares 7'' x 7'', then cut each square in half diagonally.

Cut each square diagonally.

Background fabric

▪ Cut 1 square 7½'' x 7½''.

Binding fabric

▪ Cut binding as needed for your preferred binding method.

Purchased doily (if you are not stitching out the embroidered design)

▪ If you purchased a doily, fold it in half and put seam sealant or fray preventive along the center fold. Let dry, and cut in half along the fold.

Assembly
EMBROIDERY

Pansies

1. Prepare the organza or organdy by treating it with a liquid stabilizer (see page 39). If you choose to use heavy-weight water-soluble stabilizer under the organza, make sure both stabilizer and fabric are firmly secured in the hoop.

2. Stitch out 8 pansies, remembering to cut the jump stitches between colors. Pansies grow in just about every conceivable color combination, so let your imagination run wild.

Stitch pansies on organza.

Seal edges before cutting.

Use a stencil burner to remove and seal edges.

Patty's Pointers

To ensure success with this embroidery, make sure your bobbin case is free of lint, use a new, large-eye needle, and check that your thread is feeding freely.

Hoop as many times as needed for a total of 8 pansies. You might be able to stitch as many as 4 pansies in 1 hooping.

3. After you have stitched out the pansies, stitch out 2 leaves.

4. When you have completed all embroideries, remove the fabric from the hoop, and snip all top and bobbin jump stitches. Remove excess stabilizer as necessary.

5. Use one of the following two methods for cutting out the embroideries:

   Use seam sealant or fray preventive on the edge of the flowers and leaves, and cut away the excess fabric with scissors.
   OR
   Use a wood-burning tool or a stencil burner. Organza and organdy are synthetics, so they melt when heated. Using heat to remove the embroideries is quick and seals the edge of the embroidery at the same time.

6. If you used a water-soluble stabilizer, soak your pansies to remove the stabilizer. If you leave a bit of stabilizer in the pansy, the embroidery will remain a little stiff, allowing you to shape the flowers as desired.

Doilies

1. To stitch out the doily, hoop the water-soluble stabilizer. If you have heavyweight stabilizer, 1 layer is enough; otherwise, use 2 layers of stabilizer.

2. Use the same cotton thread in the top and in the bobbin. If you are using a heavyweight thread (e.g., 30-weight), use a large needle, such as a size 100 topstitch needle. The pictured doily was made with 50-weight thread, giving the doily a nice feel.

3. Take one stitch and pull the bobbin thread to the top of the stabilizer. Hold the thread tails, and take a few stitches. Trim both thread tails. Beware: With an open design like this, it is very apparent should the thread tails become stitched within the design. Continue stitching the doily.

Doily Half stitched on water-soluble stabilizer

4. If you are stitching the *Doily Half,* you are done. If you are stitching the *Doily Quarter,* stitch it out 2 times. Cut the 2 quarters so there is about ¼'' of stabilizer left around the entire perimeter of the design. Carefully butt, but do not overlap, the two sides together, and pin in place. Use a very short, narrow zigzag stitch to sew over both motifs, adjusting the width if necessary.

5. Soak the doily in warm water to remove the stabilizer. Sometimes, rubbing the doily between your hands accelerates the process. Rinse and let air-dry. Press. (If the threads still feel stiff, repeat the process until the stabilizer is completely washed away.)

Butt doily edges, and sew using a narrow zigzag stitch.

QUILT ASSEMBLY

Use a scant ¼'' seam allowance, unless otherwise noted.

1. Fold each triangle in half along the longest side to find the center. Find the center of each side of the 7½'' square. Match the centers of 2 triangles with the centers of the opposite sides of the square. The ends of the triangles will extend past the ends of the square. Do *not* trim the triangles. Sew the triangles to the square. Press the seam allowance toward the triangles. Trim off the "dog ears" so the edges are even. Repeat with the remaining 2 triangles. The triangles are larger than the square, so the center diamond will appear to float.

2. Fold the quilt top in half, so the crease is parallel to the top and bottom edges. With your fingernail or a warm iron, gently press a crease at the center point for about 6'' along both ends of the fold. Repeat this process by folding the opposite direction, this time creating a crease parallel to both side edges.

Fold the quilt top in quarters. Center doily along creases, and sew along curved edge.

3. Spray the back of the doily with temporary spray adhesive. Center the doily on the background fabric, placing the straight edge along the horizontal crease. Place stabilizer under the fabric, and use a decorative stitch and decorative thread to sew along the curved bottom edge. Remove the stabilizer when done.

4. Layer, baste, and quilt.

5. Square up the quilt using a large square ruler and a rotary cutter.

6. Bind the quilt.

7. Position the pansies and leaves to look like a posy on the doily.

8. Pin pansies into place. Drop the feed dogs on your machine. (Stitching with the feed dogs down may take a little practice, but it will be much easier to follow the curves of the flowers and leaves.) Choose either monofilament thread or thread that matches the flowers. Use a narrow zigzag stitch to tack down all the flowers and leaves. Trim all the threads.

Position the pansies.

Stitch down the pansies.

Redwork, Bluework, and Brightwork Quilt

Made by Patty Albin

Finished quilt size:
25" x 25"

One creative way to incorporate embroideries into quilts is to *replace* part of the traditional quilt block with embroidery designs. If you look at blocks in this quilt, you can see that the design is based on a Missouri Puzzle block (see page 12). Some of the pieces within the block were replaced with embroidery.

Although the color red is traditional in a quilt like this, you can use blue or even bright colors. Pick your favorite colors to make this *your* quilt.

Supplies

See pages 36–46 for a complete description of embroidery supplies.

FABRICS

❏ 2¼ yards neutral color for embroidery backgrounds, blocks, and backing

❏ ½ yard red, blue, or bright for blocks

❏ ½ yard corresponding fabric for outer border

❏ ⅛ yard for inner border

❏ ¼ yard for binding

THREAD ORDER

LAUREL LEAVES RW
86.7mm x 86.3mm • 4,517 stitches

NOTIONS

- ❑ 50-weight cotton thread for quilt construction
- ❑ Embroidery sewing machine needles
- ❑ Tear-away stabilizer to use under the fabric
- ❑ 30-weight cotton thread for embroideries
- ❑ Hoop to accommodate a 100mm x 100mm design (If your hoop size is smaller, you will need to make size adjustments to the design.)

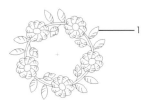

WREATH RW
86.8mm x 84.4mm • 4,671 stitches

EMBROIDERY

- ❑ *Laurel Leaves* RW, *Wreath* RW, *Branches* RW, *Basket* RW, *Frame* RW, and *Flowers* RW embroideries, transferred from the CD to a card or disk for your machine

Cutting

Background fabric

- Cut 3 strips 1⅞" x width of the fabric; then cut into 54 squares 1⅞" x 1⅞". Cut each square in half diagonally.
- Cut 1 rectangle 30" x width of the fabric for backing.
- Cut 1 strip 18" x width of the fabric for test stitching the embroideries (see page 48).
- The remaining fabric is for the embroideries.

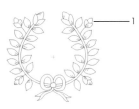

BRANCHES RW
86.4mm x 86.9mm • 4,107 stitches

Red, blue, or bright fabric

- Cut 3 strips 1⅞" x width of the fabric; then cut into 54 squares 1⅞" x 1⅞". Cut each square in half diagonally.
- Cut 3 strips 1½" x width of the fabric; then cut into 36 rectangles 2½" x 1½".

BASKET RW
79.1mm x 87mm • 5,247 stitches

Inner border fabric

- Cut 2 strips 1" x 18½" for side inner borders.
- Cut 2 strips 1" x 19½" for top and bottom inner borders.

Outer border fabric

- Cut 2 strips 3½" x 19½" for side outer borders.
- Cut 2 strips 3½" x 25½" for top and bottom outer borders.

FRAME RW
86.8mm x 85.3mm • 4,777 stitches

Binding fabric

- Cut binding as needed for your preferred binding method.

FLOWERS RW
86mm x 86.9mm • 6,046 stitches

BLUEWORK made by Gwen Woodard.

Assembly

EMBROIDERY

1. Hoop the background fabric with the tear-away stabilizer. Stitch out 9 embroideries on the background fabric. Space the embroideries so that each can be cut out in a 4½" x 4½" square.

2. When the stitching is complete, remove the stabilizer and press each embroidery before cutting.

3. Cut out each embroidery, centering it in a 4½" x 4½" square.

QUILT ASSEMBLY

Use a scant ¼" seam allowance, unless otherwise noted.

1. Sew together 1 triangle of red, blue, or bright and 1 of white to make 108 A units. Press the seam allowance toward the dark fabric.

Unit A

Make 108.

2. Sew 1 A unit to each side of a 2½" x 1½" rectangle for 36 C units.

Unit C

Make 36.

3. Attach 1 C unit to opposite sides of the embroidered squares.

Sew C units to embroidered squares.

4. Sew 1 A unit to each side of the remaining C units.

Sew A units to C unit.

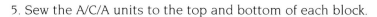

5. Sew the A/C/A units to the top and bottom of each block.

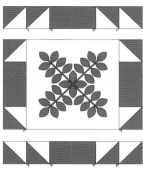

Sew A/C/A units to blocks.

6. Arrange 3 rows of 3 blocks. Sew the blocks into rows. Press the seam allowances for the blocks in adjacent rows in opposite directions so they nest when the rows are sewn together.

7. Sew the rows together. Press the seams in one direction.

8. For the inner border, sew the 18½"-long strips to each side of the quilt top. Press. Sew the 19½"-long strips to the top and bottom of the quilt top. Press.

9. For the outer border, sew the 19½"-long strips to each side of the quilt top. Press. Sew the 25½"-long strips to the top and bottom of the quilt top. Press.

10. Layer, baste, and quilt. The pictured quilts are stitched in-the-ditch along the seamlines of the Redwork patches and then the Redwork blocks.

11. Square up the quilt using a large square ruler and a rotary cutter.

12. Bind the quilt.

BRIGHTWORK made by Gwen Woodard.

Sew the rows together.

Double Wedding Ring

Made by Patty Albin

Finished quilt sizes:
23½" x 23½" or 28" x 28"

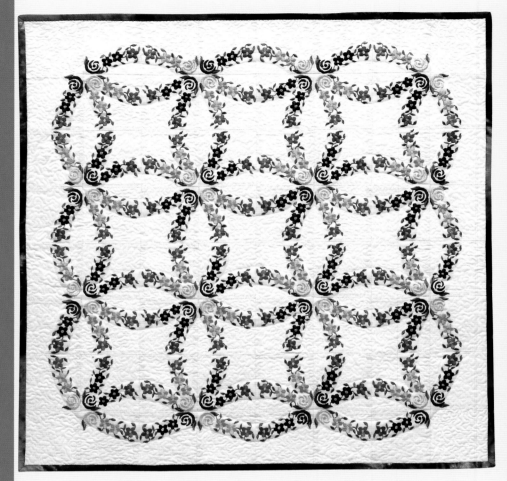

This is the best way to make a Double Wedding Ring quilt—no arcs to piece, no curved seams! After you embroider the blocks, assemble them in straight rows with straight seams.

Before you begin, you need to make a couple decisions—what size hoop to use (which determines the finished size of the quilt) and whether you want the rings to be a single color or multicolored (see photos on pages 71–72 for the differences).

Be sure to follow the directions for your hoop size (100mm or 150mm). The 150mm embroidery hoop allows you to stitch the four inner arcs of the rings at the same time in a 6" block, without re-hooping, but you will end up with a smaller quilt (23½" x 23½"). The 100mm hoop uses more blocks and makes a slightly larger quilt (28" x 28").

Please read the project guidelines on pages 48–49 before beginning the project.

Supplies

See pages 36–46 for a complete description of embroidery supplies.

FABRICS

4" embroidery (100mm hoop)

❑ 5 yards for embroidery backgrounds and backing

❑ ¼ yard for binding

❑ 34" x 34" cotton batting

6" embroidery (150mm hoop)

❑ 3½ yards for embroidery backgrounds and backing

❑ ¼ yard for binding

❑ 30" x 30" cotton batting

NOTIONS

❑ 50-weight cotton thread for quilt construction

❑ Embroidery sewing machine needles

❑ Tear-away stabilizer to use under the fabric

❑ Assorted rayon or other decorative threads for embroidery

❑ Hoop to accommodate a 100mm x 100mm design (for 4" blocks) or a 150mm x 150mm design (for 6" blocks) (If your hoop size is smaller than 100mm, you will need to make adjustments to the designs.)

EMBROIDERY DESIGNS

❑ For 4" multicolored blocks: *4mult inner* and *4mult border*

❑ For 4" single-color blocks: *4sing inner* and *4sing border*

❑ For 6" multicolored blocks: *6mult inner* and *6mult border*

❑ For 6" single-color blocks: *6sing inner* and *6sing border*

THREAD ORDER

4MULT INNER
99.3mm x 99.4mm • 6,355 stitches

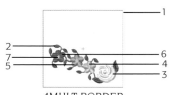

4MULT BORDER
99.3mm x 99.4mm • 3,992 stitches

4SING INNER
99.3mm x 99.4mm • 6,352 stitches

4SING BORDER
99.3mm x 99.4mm • 3,991 stitches

6MULT INNER
139.9mm x 139.8mm • 22,265 stitches

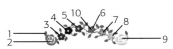

6MULT BORDER
140mm x 40.7mm • 6,718 stitches

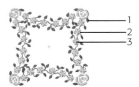

6SING INNER
140mm x 139.8mm • 22,196 stitches

6SING BORDER
140mm x 40.7mm • 6,714 stitches

NOTE: Follow the charts on pages 70–72 for the quilt you are going to make to determine how many designs you need to embroider. Some of the border designs may need to be reversed, so pay particular attention to how the designs are positioned on the quilt.

NOTE: For cutting-orientation purposes, the 4" designs have a basting line programmed into the embroidery around the design. Use this basting line when positioning your ruler to trim down your embroideries. When stitching this line, match the thread to the color of your fabric to avoid having to remove the basting line. If you choose to leave the basting line and the thread doesn't match your fabric, the thread may shadow through the seams onto your quilt top.

Cutting

Background fabric (for both sizes)

- Cut 18" x width of the fabric for test stitching the embroideries (see page 48).

For 4" blocks

- Cut 1 square 34" x 34" for the backing.
- Cut 4 squares 4" x 4" for the corners.
- The remaining fabric is for the embroideries. (You may want to cut the fabric into strips wide enough to fit in your hoop.)

For 6" blocks

- Cut 1 square 30" x 30" for the backing.
- Cut 4 squares 4" x 4" for the corners.
- The remaining fabric is for the embroideries. (You may want to cut the fabric into strips wide enough to fit in your hoop.)

Binding fabric

- Cut binding as needed for your preferred binding method.

Assembly

EMBROIDERY

1. Hoop the background fabric with the tear-away stabilizer. Stitch out the embroideries, spacing them so that each can be cut out in the appropriate-size square or rectangle.

2. When the stitching is complete, remove the stabilizer and press each embroidery before cutting.

3. Cut out each embroidery as indicated on the trimming chart (Pages 70–72) for the quilt you are making. Refer to the cutting instructions and illustrations that follow.

   For the 6" border arc, position the ruler to cut a rectangle 4" x 6", as shown below.

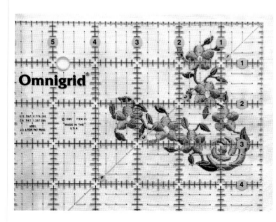

4" block: Position the basting line just on the inside of the 4"-square markings on your ruler.

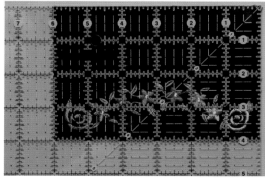

6" block: Cut the border block, factoring in a ¼" seam allowance around the embroidery on 3 sides of the block.

QUILT ASSEMBLY

Use a scant ¼" seam allowance, unless otherwise noted.

1. Arrange the ring and border pieces on a design wall. Make sure the blocks are in the proper orientation and color placement. Place the 4 plain squares in the 4 corners.

2. Sew the blocks together into rows. Press the seam allowances for the blocks in adjacent rows in opposite directions so they nest when the rows are sewn together.

3. Sew the rows together. Press the seams in one direction.

4. Layer, baste, and quilt. To enhance the illusion of the interlocking rings, quilt around the ring. Stipple quilting in the background will make the rings even more pronounced.

5. Square up the quilt using a large square ruler and a rotary cutter.

6. Bind the quilt.

Quilting

Patty's Pointers

¼" seam allowances vary from machine to machine. To make the rings smooth and continuous, you may need to adjust your seam allowance so the embroideries just touch. Check your seam allowance when you sew the first blocks together and adjust if necessary. Use the same allowance throughout the construction of this quilt.

EMBROIDERY DESIGNS AND TRIMMING

4" MULTICOLOR BLOCK	EMBROIDERY	TRIMMING
Warm colors – inner arc	Make 18 **4mult inner**	Trim to 4" x 4"
Warm colors – border arcs	Make 6 **4mult border**	Trim to 4" x 4"
Warm colors – border arcs	Make 6 **4mult border** *reversed* ◈	Trim to 4" x 4"
Cool colors – inner arc	Make 18 **4mult inner**	Trim to 4" x 4"
Cool colors – border arcs	Make 6 **4mult border**	Trim to 4" x 4"
Cool colors – border arcs	Make 6 **4mult border** *reversed* ◈	Trim to 4" x 4"

4" SINGLE-COLOR BLOCK	EMBROIDERY	TRIMMING
Warm colors – inner arc	Make 16 **4sing inner**	Trim to 4" x 4"
Warm colors – border arcs	Make 8 **4sing border**	Trim to 4" x 4"
Warm colors – border arcs	Make 8 **4sing border** *reversed* ◈	Trim to 4" x 4"
Cool colors – inner arc	Make 20 **4sing inner**	Trim to 4" x 4"
Cool colors – border arcs	Make 4 **4sing border**	Trim to 4" x 4"
Cool colors – border arcs	Make 4 **4sing border** *reversed* ◈	Trim to 4" x 4"

6" MULTICOLOR BLOCK	EMBROIDERY	TRIMMING
Inner arc	Make 9 **6mult inner**	Trim to 6" x 6"
Border arc	Make 6 **4mult border** colors from cool to warm	Trim to 4" x 6"
Border arc	Make 6 **4mult border** *reversed* ◈ colors from warm to cool	Trim to 4" x 6"

◈ = Reverse

4" Multicolor block

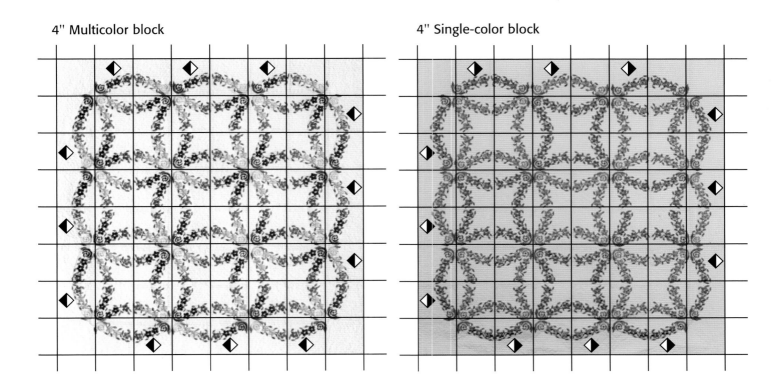

4" Single-color block

6" Multicolor block

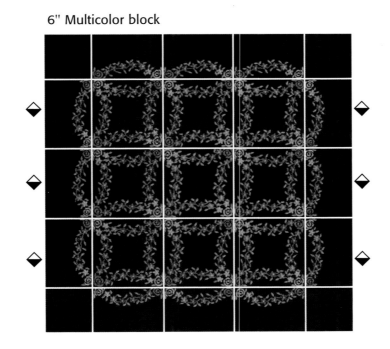

EMBROIDERY DESIGNS AND TRIMMING

6" Single-color block

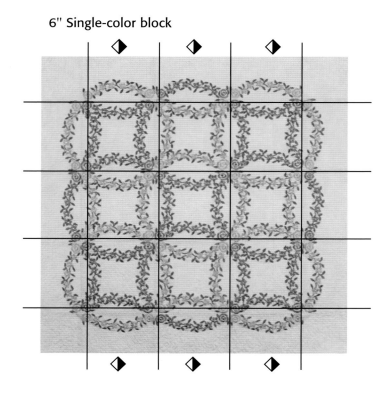

6" SINGLE-COLOR BLOCK		EMBROIDERY	TRIMMING
Warm colors – inner arc		Make 4 **6sing inner**	Trim to 6" x 6"
Warm colors – border arc		Make 8 **6sing border**	Trim to 4" x 6"
Cool colors – inner arc		Make 5 **6sing inner**	Trim to 6" x 6"
Cool colors – border arc		Make 4 **6sing border**	Trim to 4" x 6"

Miniature Baltimore Album

Made by Patty Albin

Finished quilt size:
17¼" x 17¼"

If you've always wanted to make a Baltimore Album quilt, this project is for you. Not only will you learn to make and finish a Baltimore Album quilt, you will also learn to hoop fabric so the embroidery design is stitched precisely where you want it. I call this "precision hooping."

Supplies

See pages 36–46 for a complete description of embroidery supplies.

FABRICS

- ❏ 2½ yards cream or ivory for embroidery background and backing
- ❏ ¼ yard red for binding
- ❏ 21" x 21" cotton batting

NOTIONS

- ❏ Water-soluble pen or other marker that washes away completely
- ❏ 50-weight cotton thread for quilt construction
- ❏ Embroidery sewing machine needles
- ❏ Tear-away stabilizer to use under the fabric
- ❏ Assorted rayon or other decorative threads for embroidery
- ❏ Hoop to accommodate a 100mm x 100mm design (If your hoop size is smaller, you will need to make size adjustments to the design. If you have a larger hoop, you can combine designs when stitching.)

THREAD ORDER

LAUREL LEAVES
82.6mm x 82.2mm
11,423 stitches

WREATH
83.1mm x 83.1mm
7,594 stitches

BRANCHES
83.6mm x 83.5mm • 6,897 stitches

BASKET
76.6mm x 84.3mm • 8,498 stitches

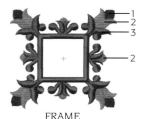

FRAME
87mm x 86.9mm • 7,737 stitches

FLOWERS
85.4mm x 85.7mm • 12,099 stitches

SWAG
38.9mm x 95.5mm
2,765 stitches

CORNER SWAG
49.2mm x 48.5mm
1,813 stitches

EMBROIDERY

☐ *Laurel Leaves*, *Wreath*, *Branches*, *Basket*, *Frame*, *Flowers*, *Swag*, and *Corner Swag* embroideries, transferred from the CD to a card or disk for your machine

☐ Optional, for the center of the *Frame* block: A monogram embroidery design, measuring 20mm or less, or a purchased ready-made appliqué

☐ Optional, if you are re-hooping the *Swag* embroidery for the border: Hoop placement template, or 4" x 4" piece of template plastic on which you have traced the *Swag* outline and placement lines (see page 77).

Cutting

Cream or ivory background fabric

■ Cut 18" x width of the fabric for test stitching the embroideries (see page 48).

■ Cut 1 square 21" x 21" for the backing.

■ Cut 4 rectangles 10" x 15" for the borders.

■ The remaining fabric is for the embroideries.

Binding fabric

■ Cut binding as needed for your preferred binding method.

Assembly

EMBROIDERY

Album Blocks

1. Hoop the background fabric with the tear-away stabilizer. Stitch out 9 Album block embroideries on the background fabric (not including the *Swag* embroideries). Space the embroideries so that each can be cut out in a 4¼" x 4¼" square.

2. When stitching is complete, remove the stabilizer, and press each embroidery before cutting.

3. Cut out each embroidery, centering it in a 4¼" x 4¼" square.

NOTE: One of the album blocks is the *Frame* design. Some embroidery machines allow you to combine designs and stitch them out together. If your machine has this feature and you want to make your quilt more personal, program a monogram initial in the center of the *Frame* embroidery design. Or, if you prefer, purchase an appliqué, and stitch it on later.

SWAG BORDERS

If you have a hoop that can accommodate a 12''-long embroidery design, you can combine 3 *Swags* end to end. Your finished embroidery should measure **exactly** 11¼'' long. You can combine these designs in your computer software or directly on your sewing machine, if it has the capability to do so. Stitch out 4 borders, each with 3 *Swags*.

If your largest hoop size is 100mm x 100mm, use the following instructions to place the *Swags* accurately when you reposition your hoop.

1. Use a water-soluble marker to draw a vertical line lengthwise down the center of 4 rectangles 10'' x 15''.

2. Draw a horizontal placement line in the center of this strip. The center placement for the first *Swag* is where the lines intersect.

3. Place the hoop with its top and bottom and horizontal positioning points on the guidelines marked on the fabric. Hoop the fabric and stabilizer together.

4. Place the hoop in the machine, with the needle positioned exactly at the intersection of the two guidelines.

5. Stitch out 1 *Swag*. Remove it from the hoop, and remove the stabilizer.

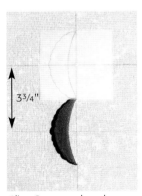

Align *Swags* and mark horizontal positioning lines.

6. Position the template plastic with the *Swag* drawn on it so the vertical positioning line lies **exactly** on the line you drew on the fabric. Make sure the tip of the *Swag* **just** touches the previously sewn *Swag*. Draw a horizontal line on the fabric where the horizontal positioning line is marked on the template. This new horizontal line should measure 3¾'' (96mm) from the previously drawn center line of the *Swag* just stitched.

7. Hoop the fabric and another piece of stabilizer together. Carefully place the hoop on the new positioning lines on your fabric. Align both horizontal and vertical guidelines with those on the hoop.

Re-hoop for next *Swag*.

NOTE: Most machines have a button or tab that allows you to move an embroidery design to an exact position. Accuracy in hooping is important for the needle to be close to the center. These adjustments allow you to place the embroidery precisely. For example, if your hooping isn't perfect, these buttons give you another chance to place the embroidery exactly where you want it.

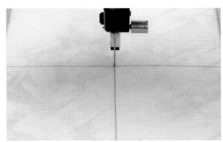

Align hooped fabric so needle is positioned exactly at the center mark.

Patty's Pointers

After stitching each *Swag*, I remove the stabilizer. I find that using one long piece of stabilizer may distort the fabric, so I always remove the stabilizer and re-hoop with a new piece.

NOTE: Do not draw all the alignment lines before you embroider. The fabric may distort and draw up when you stitch the first design. Always mark the next placement lines after you embroider the previous design.

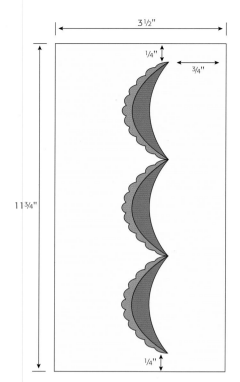

3½"

¼"

¾"

11¾"

¼"

Trim *Swag* borders.

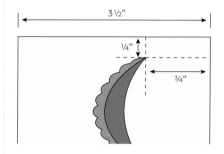

3½"

¼"

¾"

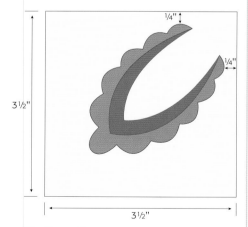

¼"

¼"

3½"

3½"

Trim *Corner Swag*.

8. Stitch out the *Swag*, remove from the hoop, and remove the stabilizer.

9. Repeat the positioning process on the other side of the first *Swag*, align the designs, mark the horizontal positioning lines, and precisely hoop the fabric. The final stitched design should measure 11¼" from tip to tip.

10. Repeat steps 2–9 three more times. You should now have 4 borders of 3 *Swags*, each embroidered end to end. Press.

11. Trim each *Swag* border rectangle to 3½" x 11¾", as shown at left.

SWAG CORNERS

1. Hoop background fabric with tear-away stabilizer. Stitch out 4 *Corner Swags*. Space the embroideries so that each can be cut out in a 3½" x 3½" square.

2. When the stitching is complete, remove the stabilizer and press each embroidery before cutting.

3. Cut out each *Corner Swag* embroidery, positioning as shown.

QUILT ASSEMBLY

Use a scant ¼" seam allowance unless otherwise noted.

1. Arrange 3 rows of 3 embroidery blocks. Sew the blocks into rows. Press the seam allowances for the blocks in adjacent rows in opposite directions so they nest when the rows are sewn together.

2. Sew the rows together. Press the seams in one direction.

3. Sew a *Swag* border to each side of the quilt top. Press.

4. Sew a *Corner Swag* block to each end of the remaining 2 *Swag* borders. Sew the borders to the top and bottom of the quilt. Press.

Seam allowance should be adjusted so the embroideries just touch.

5. Layer, baste, and quilt. Stitch in-the-ditch along all seamlines. You can also quilt around each embroidery design.

6. Square up the quilt using a large square ruler and a rotary cutter.

7. Bind the quilt.

Quilt Assembly Diagram

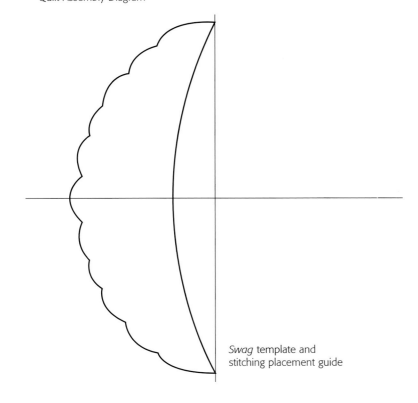

Swag template and stitching placement guide

At the time of publication, the following suppliers offered the listed products and services. While it is impossible to mention all available suppliers, I've listed some of my favorites and those with designs or patterns mentioned in this book.

SEWING MACHINE COMPANIES

To find a dealer near you, consult your local phone book or use the information listed below.

Bernina of America
www.berninausa.com
630-978-2500

Brother
www.brother.com
800-4-A-Brother

Husqvarna Viking
www.husqvarnaviking.com
800-358-0001
info@husqvarnaviking.com

Janome
www.janome.com
800-631-0183

Pfaff
www.pfaffusa.com
440-808-6550

Singer
www.singershop.com
800-4-Singer

EMBROIDERY DESIGN COMPANIES

Many of the designs shown in this book can be purchased from your local sewing machine dealer or their website. To locate a dealer near you, consult your local phone book or use the information listed above.

Embroidery designs from other sources can be purchased directly from websites.

Cactus Punch
www.cactuspunch.com
800-487-6972

Decker Design Studio
www.deckerdesignstudio.com

Embroidery Arts
www.embroideryarts.com
888-238-1372
intararts@earthlink.net

EZ Sew Designs
www.ezsew.com

Janny Primrose
www.alltronics.com.au/jpdesigns/

Jenny Haskins
www.jennyhaskins.com

Kano, designs by Karen Hinrichs
www.ericas.com/embdesigns/kano.htm to order designs

Martha Pullen
www.marthapullen.com
800-547-4176 ext. 2

Pollard's Sew Creative
www.pollardsewcreative.com
626-335-2770

Scrigby's Designs
www.scrigbys.com

Sew Artfully Yours,
Designs by Cindy Losekamp
www.sewartfullyyours.com
812-637-0697
info@sewingart.com

OTHER HELPFUL WEBSITES

The websites of the listed resources provide a wealth of information. In addition, I find these two sites helpful:

www.embroidery.com
www.annthegran.com

THREAD MANUFACTURERS

Madeira
www.madeirausa.com
800-225-3001

Mettler
www.amefird.com/mettler.htm

Robison-Anton
www.robison-anton.com
201-941-0500

Sulky of America
www.sulky.com
941-743-4634

Superior Threads
www.superiorthreads.com
800-499-1777

STABILIZERS

Stabilizers can be purchased at stores that sell fabrics and/or sewing machines.

SOFTWARE COMPANIES

Embroidery software is available from the sewing machine manufacturers and their dealers, as well as:

Buzz Tools
www.buzztools.com
fax: 800-850-2844

Origins
www.originssoftware.com
866-678-7638

OESD
www.embroideryonline.com
800-580-8885

BOOKS AND PATTERNS

Baltimore in Bloom by Pam Bono
Pam Bono Designs
800-970-5426
For purchase, contact your local Husqvarna Viking or Pfaff dealer.

Love and a Little Lunacy by Judith Hughes Marte for Around the Block Designs
2710 W. Midwick Avenue
Spokane, WA 99205
509-326-0302

P.S. I Love You by Nancy Smith and Lynda Milligan of Possibilities.
www.greatamericanquilt.com
800-474-2665

Nana's Garden by Mackie née Jeanne Gretton, quilt design by Sharon Woo for Quilt in a Day Publications
www.quiltinaday.com
800-777-4852

MACHINE EMBROIDERY SUPPLIES

Viking Distributing Company, Inc.
685 Market Street
Medford, OR 97504
800-428-2804
viking@vikingmedford.com
For stabilizers, design cards, threads, software, Sylvia Design sewing cabinets, Laurastar ironing products

QUILTING SUPPLIES

Cotton Patch Mail Order
3405 Hall Lane, Dept. CTB
Lafayette, CA 94549
800-835-4418
925-283-7883
quiltusa@yahoo.com
www.quiltusa.com

Note: Fabrics used in the quilts shown in this book may not currently be available because fabric manufacturers keep most fabrics in print for only a short time.

About the Author

Patty Albin has been an avid quilter for more than twenty years and has always loved the look of traditional quilts. With the advent of twenty-first-century sewing machines and the creative opportunities that preprogrammed machine embroideries offer, she's become passionate about incorporating these designs into her quilts, as well as showing others how to do so.

Formerly, Patty owned a quilt shop and was an associate editor of *Quiltmaker* magazine. Currently, she is a freelance teacher, an AQS Certified Quilt Appraiser, and a Husqvarna Viking Educator. Patty is working with Husqvarna Viking to design embroidery cards. She also has a signature line of fabrics with Erlanger Fabrics.

From *Beautiful Baltimore* embroidery designs by Patty Albin from Husqvarna Viking

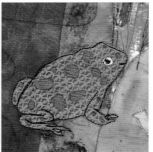

HOW TO USE THE CD

1. Place the enclosed CD in your computer CD drive.
2. Click (highlight) the folder on the CD that contains the designs in the format used by your embroidery machine.
3. Move or copy the folder from the CD to a folder on your computer.
4. The designs are now available to transfer to your sewing machine as you would any other purchased designs.

EMBROIDERY DESIGN SOFTWARE LICENSE

1. LICENSE: The design software is licensed to the original customer for embroidery use at one location. The use of the software at more than one location is a violation of copyright law.

2. COPYRIGHTS: The embroidery designs are owned and copyrighted by Patty Albin and are protected by United States copyright laws and international treaties. You may not copy the software except a) you may make one copy of the software for back-up or archival purposes; and b) you may transfer the software onto a hard disk, provided you keep the original solely for back-up or archival purposes.

3. OTHER RESTRICTIONS: You may not rent, lease, or share the software designs.

4. WARRANTY DISCLAIMER: C&T Publishing Inc. liability and your exclusive remedy for a defective product shall be either a) replacement of defective software; or b) a return of the purchase price paid for the returned software.

5. REPRODUCTION AND SALE OF EMBROIDERED GOODS: This license allows you to sew the designs on fabric or other material for your personal use only; you may not use these designs for any financial gain.

For additional embroidery designs by Patty Albin, look for her *Beautiful Baltimore* embroidery card by Husqvarna Viking. See Resources on page 78 for contact information.

Bonus design from the *Beautiful Baltimore* embroidery card is included on the enclosed CD!